ACPL IT

DISCARDED

S0-BFR-138

Here' ᵤt

DO NOT REMOVE
CARDS FROM POCKET

8/17/93

"Mr. Dayley has written a very readable book that guides the reader step-by-step through the major issues that an entrepreneur should address in raising capital for his or her business, as well as in using the SCOR procedure for this purpose. It should prove useful to lawyers, accountants and other advisers to small businesses, as well as to the entrepreneurs themselves."

Mike Liles Jr.
Lawyer and creator of the first SCOR documents in 1986
Bogle & Gates
Seattle, Washington

"It was a very easy book to read and quite informative. My first thoughts would be that I wish I had this book three years ago when I decided to start this company. It sure would have saved a lot of time and grief in finding investors. I wasted hours on SBA loans and banks. . . . I would definitely recommend this book for any person considering starting up a new company, not only as a way to finance a new company, but definitely as a guide on how not to waste valuable time on certain avenues used to raise capital."

Jerilyn Koskan
Owner
Donlar Corporation
Harvey, Illinois

"James Dayley's *SCORing MILLIONS* has struck a nerve. I couldn't put it down. I have never met an entrepreneur or business owner who did not bitterly complain about the injustice of have to 'give away' so much of 'his company' just to be able to continue to work hard to make it grow. This book should be on the 'must read' list for entrepreneurs and their advisers. Dayley's step-by-step exposition of the SCOR process is a major contribution to our nation's future health. Believe it!"

Wayne C. Mosher
Business Consultant
St. Louis, Missouri

"I have found *SCORing MILLIONS* easy to read and very helpful in getting organized to raise equity capital for our expanding business. As we submit our disclosure documents, I know that the whole process would have been more costly and much more time consuming if it weren't for James Dayley's expertise. He has made what could be a confusing and complicated process understandable. It's just what we needed!"

Tim Monnig
President and CEO
Justin Entertainment, Inc.
Atlanta, Georgia

SCORING MILLIONS

James H. Dayley

AIMPress

Cover design by Lee, Allen Advertising
Edited by Kurt Wulff

Library of Congress Cataloging-in-Publication Data

Dayley, James H., 1934-

SCORing MILLIONS
James H. Dayley
p. cm.
Includes bibliographical references and index.
ISBN 1-881183-01-7

1. Going public (Securities) -- United States
2. Small business -- United States -- Finance.
I. Title.
HG4028.S7D39 1992 658.15'224--dc20 92-26508 CIP

Printed in USA

10 9 8 7 6 5 4 3 2 1

DEDICATION

▼

To Shirley, my best friend for the last 37 years, or is it 38?

To Teresa, Tami, Bret and Krista for your collective patience with your dad who, through this book, might have finally discovered what he wants to do when he grows up.

ACKNOWLEDGEMENTS

▼

Though the "Acknowledgements" in most books note the efforts of those people that worked directly on the project, I've chosen to expand my "Thanks." I believe all of the following have in some way assisted in my success and ultimately this book.

In personal development:

To all my teachers go my heartfelt thanks for a wealth of wonderful lessons taught.

To my mother and father, for bringing a new life into the world during the deep gloom of the Great Depression and instilling in me eternal values of self-worth and intrinsic excellence, tempered with hard work and love for achievement.

To my high school coach, the late Rulon Budge, for training me long before I even knew of Vince Lombardi, that the breaks come to those who block and tackle the best.

To the many instructors at various universities who allowed me the opportunity to fail and another chance when I did.

To my old comrades-in-arms of the 307th bomb wing of the Strategic Air Command where the motto "Peace is Our Profession" was daily reality.

To the other two crew members of Select Crew S-02, Jerry Laughlin and Clint Batson -- my buddies in the air as well as fellow hunters of the wily Nebraska ringneck pheasants.

To the men and their families of various U.S. Air Force organizations of which I served as commander. I especially want to thank those sergeants, with all the stripes on their sleeves, who took the "ol' man" half their age out from behind a desk to go visit various maintenance shops and stations. They were way ahead of the technique of "management-by-walking-around" before it became popular at Hewlett-Packard.

To the Assignments Division at Military Personnel Center that sent me to work on the expansion of the nation's military airlift capacity. Being a part of providing the capacity to carry out "Desert Storm" gives me great personal satisfaction. Many great management lessons were learned during those years.

In business activities:

To Gary Shaw who took a chance on a military engineer being able to make it in the investment sales business.

To Curt Kasten of Kasten Group, Inc. who took time to teach me how to evaluate businesses for possible acquisition and how to negotiate the kind of deals that got done.

Specifically having to do with the SCOR program:

To Marvin Mears and Wilma More of Corporate Capital Resources for introducing me to and tutoring me on the whole process.

To Greg Toms and Kent Fie of the State of Washington's Securities Division who took me to "ding-dong school" to learn how to get the documentation completed on Form U-7.

More specifically having to do with this SCOR book:

To Drew Field for his encouragement and expert advice on the entire process of raising public equity funds. I also extend my sincere appreciation to him for writing the Foreword for this book.

To Tony Hitt, Kurt Wulff and Lena Usery at AIM Press in St. Louis for helping to bring this book to completion.

To Tona Court and Ellen Hahn for their exceptional, and tireless, proofreading efforts and suggestions.

Contents

▼

Foreword 23

Introduction 27

SECTION ONE
Alternatives for Funding "The Entrepreneurial Dream"

Section Introduction 37

1. Friends and Relatives 41

2. Banks 45

3. SBA Loans 47

4. Private Placements 51
5. Venture Capital 55
6. Wall Street IPO's 65
7. Blind Pools & Public Shells 67

Section Summary 69

SECTION TWO
A Different Approach to Capital Formation for Small Business

Section Introduction 71

8. Funding Entrepreneurs in a Market Economy 73
9. Evolution of the SCOR Program 77

SECTION THREE
To SCOR or Not to SCOR?

Section Introduction 83

10. Profile of a Good SCOR Candidate 85
11. Applying SCOR in the Real World 89
12. Other Considerations 95
13. What It Means to Be Public 99

Section Summary

SECTION FOUR
Registering to Sell Your Company's Stock

Section Introduction 103

14. The Basic Premise 105
15. Advice Before You Get Started 109
16. Form U-7 Instructions 127
17. Form U-7 and Exhibits 151

SECTION FIVE
Selling Your Stock to the Public

Section Introduction 241

18. A Marketing Plan Approach 243

SECTION SIX
Future Considerations

Section Introduction 253

19. SCORing Again 255
20. Introducing Regulation "A" Filings 257
21. Summary & Conclusions 261
22. SCOR Checklist 265
23. Q & A 267
24. Stop the Presses! 277

North American Regulators 285

Suggested Reading 305

Index 309

Notes to the Reader

The author presents this information as a business consultant/entrepreneur with the belief that the material is both correct and timely. However, the author is neither an attorney nor a CPA. Prior to using any of this material for funding a business, the methodology should be approved by professional counsel and the appropriate federal and state governmental securities officials.

Masculine pronouns and possessives are used throughout this book to simplify communication, but the information is of equal value to men and women.

FOREWORD

Jim Dayley's book about SCOR (Small Corporate Offering Registration) reflects what comes across when you meet him -- enthusiasm, friendliness -- successfully coupled with serious determination. This last quality led Jim to me and to my own work. As Jim was researching this book, he would call me whenever he had questions or needed some insight into new information he had come upon. When Jim finally gave me a copy of the pre-publication galley and asked me to write a Foreword, I read it cover to cover. Then I gladly accepted the job. *SCORing MILLIONS* is just the kind of "how-to" resource that entrepreneurs need -- right now!

I've been through a successful million-dollar SCOR public offering, and I'm in the midst of advising companies on others. My experience as a securities lawyer for entrepreneurs raising capital in public share offerings goes back over 30 years. It led me to write my own book on the public offering process, published in 1991.

One very clear and strong conclusion comes from those years of experience: Entrepreneurs have to take personal responsibility for their own companies' capital formation. There is no way to turn it all over to some commissioned intermediary.

Raising capital needs to become another major part of the ongoing business, just like sales, people management, and accounting. That means the entrepreneur has to be personally involved on a daily basis. That calls for being informed. *SCORing MILLIONS* informs entrepreneurs on one of the most revolutionary opportunities to hit small business in decades.

There are three integral parts to the book that every entrepreneur should carefully study:

1. The various alternatives for financing a growing business. Jim gives you the hard truth and myths behind venture capital, bank loans, borrowing from family and friends, as well as other previously touted sources.

2. What not to do. You'll gain from the costly experience of others, saving you the potential grief from making the same mistakes.

3. How to speed up the process for raising capital from a SCOR offering, without getting bogged down in detail and running headlong into dead ends.

Jim deals with a very specific new tool, the Small Corporate Offering Registration. This is the perfect fit for entrepreneurs with businesses that could use up to $1 million to take on new and exciting challenges.

Your experience with SCOR will also give you the knowledge and confidence needed to move into further rounds of capital formation through public share offerings. During 1992, the U.S. Securities and Exchange Commission adopted the U-7 format (form for SCOR) for offerings of up to $5 million. It has proposed making that same procedure available for even broader registration and reporting for any company with less than $25 million in annual revenues.

This book will give you a foundation in SCOR that will carry over while you raise greater amounts of money from new shareowners, taking advantage of the continuing expansion of the SCOR process. If you have a business that needs money to grow -- money that comes without a repayment date or an interest rate, or restrictions on how you can run your business -- then you've come to the right place. Read Jim Dayley's *SCORing MILLIONS* and best of luck in all your business ventures.

- Drew Field
Author of "Take Your Company Public!"

INTRODUCTION

▼

Sometimes good things happen to those who wait, but, in general, entrepreneurs and their small companies don't have much staying power. For instance, it never ceases to amaze me how bankers say that a particular business that went bankrupt wasn't a good business or that the owner was inept. My reply to such statements is best served by a simple analogy.

Take three little plants that you would buy at the local garden shop. Place them in a good sunny spot on your patio. For all intents and purposes, they all three look the same. Now, if you were to water and fertilize two of the three, what would happen? Well, the answer would be that two would flourish and the other one would eventually die. So, the next question would be, "Was it just a bad plant?" The answer is that we'll never know. It just didn't get enough nourishment!

Break. Break.

I like entrepreneurs. I like everything about them -- their high energy levels; their dissatisfaction with the status quo; their unorthodox methods of operating; their propensity for action -- all of those characteristics and temperaments. My self-imposed mission in life is to help entrepreneurs like you obtain the "nourishment" that will enable you to fulfill your business and personal dreams.

This book will help fulfill the mission. It contains the recipe for an entrepreneur to seize the opportunity -- to become financially independent by carefully growing and developing a business. How? As an entrepreneur, what could you do with $1 million -- not as a loan, but as an equity investment in you and your company? Putting your response into action is the essence of this book. I came across the basic concepts involved with a way to do such a thing in August of 1990. If you properly utilize the various ingredients involved, you can embark upon a newly blazed trail to monetary security.

You can obtain the money necessary to fulfill your dreams through a process called SCOR, which stands for Small Corporate Offering Registration. In some states it's called ULOR, which stands for Uniform Limited Offering Registration. It's a method for obtaining money from small investors. Yes, by using this process, owners of small businesses can sell some of their company's stock to the general public.

I'd been working through the learning process on the SCOR program for over a year prior to attending the U.S. Securities and Exchange Commission's Forum on Small Business Capital Formation held in Washington, D. C. in late 1991. Afterward, I spent several months meeting with lawyers, accountants, bankers, and entrepreneurs in an effort to promote the SCOR program. I explained to anyone who would listen how a small company could sell up to $1 million of their stock to the general public. Most people were interested in a new idea, but didn't know what it might mean to them or their clients. More specifically then, what could SCOR mean to you?

Let's start with some examples of how entrepreneurs have been able to obtain money for their dreams. Over 20 years ago, Dan Evins started a chain of home cookin'/ol' country gift shop establishments. After a stint in the Marines, two years as a congressional aide to his uncle, and some time as a teller in his brother's bank, he went to work at a gasoline distributorship founded by his grandfather. He helped the company begin the transition from rural Tennessee gas stations to locations along the new interstate highways. His idea was to attract motorists by adding a home cookin' restaurant and an ol' country gift shop to the gas stations. It was 1969 when he borrowed $40,000 to start the first store. It made money the first month. Feeling he had developed a really hot idea, he wanted to expand upon it quickly. He found 10 investors to put in $10,000 each to begin the expansion. Unfortunately, the $100,000 cost him half of the original stock of his company. Today, after selling off the gas stations, there are 124 Cracker Barrel stores. The company is now worth over $1 billion and Dan Evins' diluted ownership after going public (just over 1%) is now worth $11.5 million. Sure, this is more than enough to live comfortably, but what could it have been had he not sold such a large percentage of the company?

A more recent example involves Randall Bourne and his company Exposures, Inc. He got the idea for his business after he became a father in 1982. From his experience as a photo studio operator in California in the early '70s, he knew that people take lots of pictures -- especially of their first child. He wasn't any different, except perhaps more frustrated that he couldn't find the type and quality of frames in which to display both his amateur photography and his daughter, Kirsten.

While working at an advertising agency in New York, Bourne started some in-depth research on an idea that was taking shape in his head. First, he found that Americans take 40 million photographs a day! Most find their way to a bottom drawer or into a cheap holder of some kind. Secondly, he learned that people would really like to display their photographs if there were some attractive frames for them. Finally, he found that he could penetrate a larger market nationally if he would promote frames through direct marketing. Cataloging was growing at the rate of 15% per year.

In early 1986 he quit his job! He had raised $400,000 to get started -- $40,000 of his own money and the rest from family and friends. By the time he got his first catalog out in July, he had spent over $100,000 -- 25% of the capital! However, the first mailing brought in $100,000. The second and third produced revenues of $400,000 each. This year, Exposures expects to sell $15 million worth of merchandise and net $450,000.

And now -- the rest of the story! Randall Bourne has a successful business, but he ran out of money shortly after his first mailing. His bank was both unable and unwilling to help. He got an offer from a public cataloger to buy the company for $1 million, but he wasn't interested. His next stop was at the door of some venture capitalists. He got $1.2 million, but at the cost of 80% of his company! Everyone knows 20% of something is better than 100% of nothing.

How could the new SCOR program help people like Dan Evins and Randall Bourne? First of all, it takes a lot more money to do things in 1992 than it did in 1969 or even 1986. Secondly, most entrepreneurs are not well connected to a network of private investors or venture capitalists. Finally, most companies with dynamic growth potential need to be able to raise money on a regular basis. The public market is the only place to consistently do so. Thus, through the use of the SCOR program, you may raise up to $1 million to launch or expand your business. Furthermore, you won't have to give up 50% to 80% of the company to do so.

Initially, I just couldn't believe that there was such a "ho hum" response to my SCOR story from the Washington conference. It reminded me of my first few months in the stock brokerage business in 1976. One of the brightest brokers there was selling a new product and, of all things, wasn't getting paid for it!

"Why are you doing such a thing?" I asked.

"As a broker, you always have to be prospecting for new business. I feel these new Money Market Mutual Funds will allow me to gather money. That's the direction in which the brokerage business is evolving. Most likely, some of the money I gather will eventually go into investments that I'll get paid for. If I can establish a relationship with people, I think they will invest with me when it comes time to do so rather than with my competitors."

Nobody knew much about Money Market Mutual Funds then or even seemed to care. They had many questions, such as: "How safe are they?" "How fast can I get my money out?" "How much interest do they pay?" "How does that compare to my savings account?" Eventually, billions of dollars left the banks and savings and loan companies seeking higher interest and flexibility. Hundreds of

Money Market Mutual Funds were born.

Today, almost everyone knows what a Money Market Mutual Fund is or at least has heard of them. I predict that in a few years from now, most people who know anything about general business trends will know of the SCOR Process and what it will have done to provide capital for small businesses. It will take some time to become well-known just like it did for Money Market Mutual Funds. I want to be like my associate from the brokerage business and let you in on the deal early.

I was very dissatisfied with the pace of my one-on-one presentations. I had worked on the SCOR document preparation process for five different companies. I believed in the SCOR process and wanted to make money by helping other entrepreneurs use it to fund their ventures. It seemed like I had something really great and couldn't even give it away!

It reminded me of the time I couldn't give away box seat baseball tickets. I was in Minneapolis as part of the U.S. Air Force Reliability Improvement Team working on the automatic flight control system for the C-5 aircraft. It was built by Honeywell. Late in the first day's meeting, I asked how to get to the ball park. Ted Williams was managing the visiting team, and I wanted to see him in person. I was told that a bus to the stadium stopped right out in front of my hotel. When the employee from Honeywell found out that I wanted to go to the game, he said he would get me a ticket to sit in their company box. He came back a few minutes later -- with 8 tickets in his hand!

"What am I going to do with 8 tickets?" I exclaimed.

"Well, these tickets are for our guests or employees, and since the weather's not too good, nobody's picked them up. Just take 'em and give 'em away."

A couple of hours later I was standing at the bus stop wondering what in the world I was going to do to give away these great tickets. Pretty soon the bus pulled up and I got on. Once inside, I announced that I had 7 tickets to sit in Honeywell's box if anyone wanted them. Silence! Nobody stirred! I couldn't stand it and burst out laughing. Finally, one man from this group of bleacher fans sauntered up from the back of the bus. He took one of the tickets and carefully examined it. He told me thanks as he returned to his seat. Then I was deluged! People quickly took the rest of the tickets. We all had a fun, but chilly night at the game.

So, be like the first man on the bus. Check out this SCOR deal! Why risk always being in the bleachers?

While preparing SCOR documents for filing, I hit upon the idea to do seminars on SCOR. In this way, I could get the word out faster to entrepreneurs. They needed to know this option was now available. The state of Washington had been promoting the SCOR process with seminars, so I thought people all over the country would also be interested.

One of the first seminars attracted an enthusiastic group of entrepreneurs with companies in various stages of development. After it was over, one of them, a small publishing company president, remained to talk with me. He, like the rest of the attendees, was interested in how he might raise money for his company.

Besides SCOR, he had another idea.

"If you were to write a book on SCOR, you would be able to spread the word much faster than would ever be possible with a one- man seminar tour."

I was stunned. I glanced at my seminar outline for a moment, envisioned it as the table of contents for a SCOR book, and soon countered with, "I can do that!"

That's how *SCORing MILLIONS* got started. I wanted to do all

I could to rapidly promote the SCOR program and help people work through the process.

This is an extraordinary time to have such a wonderful tool available. What! Don't I know that we're in the midst of the first real white-collar recession ever? Yes, I do, but from my understanding of contrary investment thinking, I am convinced that people will look back at 1992 as a great time to have started or expanded a business. I saw the same thing in 1982 when I was trying to get executives to acquire businesses. They wanted to "wait until things got better" and when they did the good deals weren't as prevalent.

I'm disturbed by the pessimism of this present time, yet I know it's just human nature. We fought the Cold War throughout most of my lifetime -- and we won! As a young navigator-bombardier, I sat for weeks at a time over a five-year period on alert -- big "H" bombs in our old B-47 Aircraft. I stood ready, willing and able to participate in the mass destruction of humanity. I rejoiced in September of 1991 when the crews of the Strategic Air Command were taken off Alert. I felt like I'd finally come off Alert myself.

Now it's time to pound our swords into plowshares and our spears into pruning hooks. It'll take a period of difficult transition, but it's time to move on to solving other problems. It is my firm conviction that the discipline we showed in the past to win the minds of men against communism can be applied to the other challenges of our era. I further believe small businesses, with the driving force of their dynamic entrepreneurial leaders, are the answer.

At such a great point in the world's history, it is exciting to know that there is a mechanism, a process, a methodology by which today's entrepreneurs can fulfill their dreams. These more enlightened individuals can take themselves and their employees to unequaled heights.

Please take a couple of deep breaths right here! Why? I want to let you know that IF you are really a dedicated entrepreneur, you can get all money you need to make your business a success! The key is to make steady progress on each level you attempt to climb. If you can do so, the money for the next level will be available when you need it.

The growth of a business takes money -- lots of money. Just when you think you've gotten every expense covered, new ones pop up. Leaving yourself short on cash as a company is growing is the beginning of the end. What you need to do is to obtain funds for your typical small company to begin the transition to major firm status.

The approach I've decided to use in this book is to think of you as a client who's sitting beside me at a table. Through this book, I will provide you with an overview of SCOR, and all that goes with it, so that you can effectively decide if this is an avenue that is appropriate for your company. While it is difficult, it's not nearly as intimidating when you have someone to guide you along. I compare the explanation of the SCOR process with similar problem-solving sessions I had during my time in engineering school, many years ago. My classmates and I were mature officers sent to a civilian university in mid-career to help fill the military's pressing need for engineers. We had to complete a full engineering curriculum in 27 months. We worked hard helping each other figure out the difficult problems assigned. I really enjoyed this process. I have a similar feeling about what I've been able to assimilate on this new way to raise capital for small businesses, especially at a time of such great opportunity.

So, let's get on with it! Let's start *SCORing MILLIONS.*

INTRODUCTION

SECTION ONE

Alternatives for Funding "The Entrepreneurial Dream"

This section contains various alternatives that entrepreneurs might try in order to fund their dreams. Each approach has its advantages and disadvantages. These are discussed in their individual chapters. Nevertheless, it seems appropriate that we

---

first discuss the overall advantages and disadvantages of debt (loans) versus equity (sale of company stock). The typical entrepreneur needs to understand these key items prior to looking at the various funding alternatives.

DEBT

Advantage

A company owner doesn't have to give up any ownership when getting a loan. Rather, he just has to make the prescribed payments, on time, until the loan is paid back.

Disadvantage

The debt has to be secured or collateralized so that the lender can get the amount loaned returned to him in the event of default by the borrower.

EQUITY

Advantage

When the owner sells shares in his company to someone for something of value (cash, services, merchandise, etc.), he doesn't have to pay the person back. The shareholder will now participate in the success or failure of the enterprise.

Disadvantage

You now have a person who is more than a partner -- he's got some part of your business. You can't just do what you want to do without considering his interests, because the stockholder has legal rights, even if he only holds a minority interest in the company.

As companies move through the various stages of their growth, their levels of both debt and equity are under constant review by their managements. Likewise, scrutiny by companies' lenders and stockholders is also continual. The true test of an entrepreneurial owner is mainly centered around how well he manages his company's debt to equity relationship. How well he does so is often referred to as either a clean (good) or a cluttered (bad) balance sheet for the enterprise.

1

FRIENDS & RELATIVES

▼

I recently heard the story of a man who started four businesses with four different friends. Years later, he doesn't have either the businesses OR the friends.

Nevertheless, Randall Bourne, founder of Exposures, Inc., discussed in the introduction to this book, went to his friends and relatives to get started. I'd suggest you reread his story after completing this chapter.

Advantages

It's Fast. The entrepreneur has a positive relationship with a friend or relative he approaches with the idea. Therefore, the proposal can be made quickly. It might go something like this:

"Say, Uncle Henry, I've been working on this really great idea for a business. I need about $200,000 over the next six months to get it off the ground. I've got about half of it put together from myself and my partners. If I could get you some information on the venture and you liked it, do you think you could put up the other $100,000 I need?"

It Can Be Informal. Direct personal discussions with friends and relatives allow the entrepreneur to display his in-depth knowledge of the opportunity as well as exhibit his enthusiasm with the overall project. He can use a prototype of the product or pictures of the operation in some stage of development. Getting something tangible into the prospective investors' hands is often the key to obtaining funds.

Disadvantages

Lack of Extensive Venture Investing Experiences. Most friends and relatives are not experienced in early-stage venture funding. The "rich" person's money is only part of what the entrepreneur needs. The real need is to have the aid and assistance provided by a network of professionals in the venture investing field.

Limited Financial Staying Power. Even the wealthiest friend or relative has a limited capacity to put money into a start-up or near start-up business. Invariably, unforeseen events occur and more money is required. It also seems to happen at the worst time for the "seed" investor. Unless there is unlimited potential for additional money, the entrepreneur is skating on thin ice to accept any such funding.

Less Rigorous Investment Proposal Preparation. Entrepreneurs hate to put things in writing. Nevertheless, the experience obtained through the crafting of a well-prepared investment proposal document, commonly called a business plan, is an exercise well worth the time and effort. Why? Unless the project has a good foundation, there is little hope for the venture to succeed. Without the discipline imposed by having to prepare a quality document, the venture preparation is incomplete. Too many entrepreneurs look upon the preparation of the business plan simply as a way to tell potential investors about the opportunity. Then they invariably stuff it into a file once the funding is completed. No action on the part of the entrepreneur could be more wrong! A properly crafted business plan is the "Bible" for the business. It is constantly under review and, in essence, is a living and breathing entity. It needs to be revised periodically and referred to regularly. It is the common ground upon which the goals and objectives of the enterprise are communicated both within the company and to various outsiders when appropriate.

Loss of Relationships. There is a very real possibility the relationship will be strained, at best, and destroyed, at worst, if you accept funding for your enterprise from a typical friend or relative. Why? Well, nothing ever goes exactly as planned.

Someone or someone's spouse will get disappointed with whatever the deal was or wasn't supposed to accomplish. Some degree of failure is inevitable. The best that can be hoped for is that the failure to meet stated goals and objectives is not catastrophic to the business. You then take corrective action to get it back on track again. In general, the emotional stress of the loss of a relationship is too much of a risk for most people.

RECOMMENDATION: DO NOT FUND YOUR ENTERPRISE THROUGH FRIENDS OR RELATIVES!

2

BANKS

Doesn't it seem reasonable for a person needing money to go to a bank to get it? Sure, it does! However, there's a problem. You have to prove that you have the capacity to pay the loan back out of funds not related to the enterprise you got the loan for in the first place. Banks have to act that way because their rules and regulations provide for their loans to be properly supported, or to use the banker's term -- collateralized. That's because the widows' and orphans' money on deposit in banks shouldn't be invested in risky ventures.

It's always been inappropriate for an entrepreneur to seek

venture funding at a regular bank. Today's economic situation is even more restrictive. Any entrepreneur who goes to a bank looking for venture funding is really doing himself a disservice. It discloses that he's not a well-informed individual to even seek funding from a bank.

Regardless, banks are indispensable for businesses to operate in today's economic environment. They can process your customer's checks, process wire transfers of funds, provide you with letters of credit (for instance, for an order being imported) and provide you with lines-of-credit to pay for work-in-progress. However, all of these services have to be properly paid for and/or collateralized.

One of the really tough problems banks have is with rapidly growing companies. Let's say the success of their product line is so great that current orders have expanded and new orders are rolling in. Everyone at the company is elated. Right? Sure -- until the owner goes to his bank and asks the bank to double his line-of-credit so that he can make all the new products. The bank's refusal usually leads to the company changing banks. It causes difficulties viewing you as a stable customer. The new bank likes the idea of getting a new customer from a competitor. Nevertheless, continued rapid growth will soon wear out your welcome at the second bank. You move to an even bigger bank with more capability and, of course, continued restrictions to your business' continued growth.

RECOMMENDATION: DON'T ASK BANKS FOR VENTURE CAPITAL MONEY.

3

SBA LOANS

In general, loans are exactly what a start-up or rapidly expanding company doesn't need. What such individuals and companies need is EQUITY CAPITAL! You can't borrow your way to prosperity.

In the past, Small Business Administration (SBA) loans were given to entities that had been turned down by loans by at least two banks prior to going to the SBA for help. The SBA then guaranteed or "co-signed" the loan for the borrower at a bank.

These loans are arranged under the conditions that:

1. The business activity involved is very easily classified so that the SBA personnel can check out your projections against industry norms.

2. A very routine proposal is presented to the SBA.

3. Collateral of easy conversion was provided by the borrower.

4. The loan could be serviced from the cash flow of the business with a comfortable margin for unexpected contingencies.

Things have changed at the SBA since President Reagan threatened to do away with it. It is now a much more responsive organization. For example, the SBA can now lend up to $750,000. Also, informational brochures on all sorts of business topics have been enhanced and expanded. Such information and the advice from their SCORE, Service Corps of Retired Executives, are especially helpful to young companies.

The SBA administers a conservative venture capital program through what are called Small Business Investment Companies or SBIC's. Under this program, these venture capital companies can use one dollar to gain several more dollars from the SBA. The SBIC's get their money at low rates of interest and then re-loan it to businesses at market rates. These are usually done in the form of subordinated debentures which are essentially corporate promises to repay in a specifically defined manner. Regardless, they are still loans and require collateral. The SBIC's can temper the terms on such securities, but they are generally more "debt" than "equity." Many SBIC's are affiliated with banks and, therefore, are between banks and the regular venture capital companies.

Furthermore, legislation enhancing the capacity for SBIC's to operate more aggressively in their work was recently passed by Congress and signed into law by President Bush.

RECOMMENDATION: DON'T TRY TO FUND YOUR COMPANY FROM SBA LOANS. THEY SHOULD ONLY BE USED IN CONJUNCTION WITH "REAL EQUITY," AND EVEN THEN, ONLY WHEN THERE IS NO DOUBT YOU CAN PAY THE MONEY BACK.

4

PRIVATE PLACEMENTS

This chapter is not intended or designed to be a definitive explanation of this subject. Rather, it's a layman's overview of the subject and what it means to the typical entrepreneur.

When you've "tapped out" your friends and relatives, been turned down by your bank and find SBA loans too restrictive, don't be surprised to hear your lawyer say something like, "Well, we could always try to do a private placement."

How can private placements help entrepreneurs? Funds could be raised by the sale of a "security" of the company involved. What does that mean? The company makes an "exempt offering." Such a security does not have to be fully registered with Federal or State Securities Divisions. What's involved is a way in which an offering can be made to sophisticated individuals with sizeable net worth. The whole procedure has advantages and disadvantages.

Advantages

Less Complicated Than a Public Offering. A private placement memorandum is prepared to properly disclose each and every pertinent fact about the business -- good and bad. This documentation is primarily intended for the use of "sophisticated investors" and not the general public.

Relatively Fast. Sometimes there is an informal network of individuals who invest in Private Placements. Either they like to have personal involvement with companies or just want to get in on the ground floor of something with potentially high return.

Disadvantages

Lack of Liquidity (defined as the ability to buy and sell at will). This is, by design of the exemption from registration, a mandatory condition. The investment must be made for a long period of time and is not offered or purchased with the need or intent to sell quickly. Nevertheless, no matter how sophisticated or wealthy a person, there is understandable concern with "locking up" any investment for a long period of time without even the option to sell it.

Limited Number of Potential Investors. Each state has determined just how many people can be "offered" such a security. However, the maximum number applies to the unsophisticated person and not to the person who can show high net worth and income. The individual must state in writing that if he were to lose the entire amount invested, that it would not affect his lifestyle. In spite of this, it's hard to raise such funds if a network of this kind doesn't exist.

Only Limited Amounts of Capital Can Be Raised in a Timely Manner. While big investment bankers can make huge private placements of capital and do so all the time, it is not the usual case for individual entrepreneurs or small companies. Even when the proper clearances are obtained from the State Securities Division to have individuals in the securities business help sell the private placement, it still takes a lot of time and effort. Getting $10,000 from such a person is one thing. Getting $40,000 is quite another story when you consider trying to coordinate with an accountant, a lawyer, etc.

RECOMMENDATION: DISCUSS THIS SUBJECT WITH YOUR ATTORNEY. IT'S IMPORTANT YOU UNDERSTAND IT. THE SCOR PROGRAM DISCUSSED IN THE NEXT SECTION IS ONLY MADE OPERATIONAL THROUGH A METHOD OF EXEMPTION FROM FEDERAL REGISTRATION.

5

VENTURE CAPITAL

As Senior Consultant with the now national firm called The Kasten Group, Inc., I began a dedicated search for venture capital for our clients in 1986. I was in the process of trying to find equity funding for the leveraged buy-outs of small companies. A typical deal involved an elderly owner of a business agreeing to sell for $4 million. He agreed to take back 25% of the deal, or $1 million, in the form of a promissory note. The buyer could usually get about half of the purchase price financed in some sort of asset-based financing on the accounts receivable, inventory and equipment; in this example, $2 million. So we were $1 million short. Most executive clients were able to come up with $400,000 to $500,000. Working for someone else doesn't usually allow a person to accumulate vast wealth. That's why they were trying to get a business of their own in the first place. Therefore, in order to get the deal done, we had to come up with real equity for the rest of the total selling price.

While we were able to solve these puzzles a few times, it was a real exercise in frustration. However, what came out of the exercise of searching was a clear understanding of what venture capital is and what it is not. The key was to find out what venture capital WAS NOT.

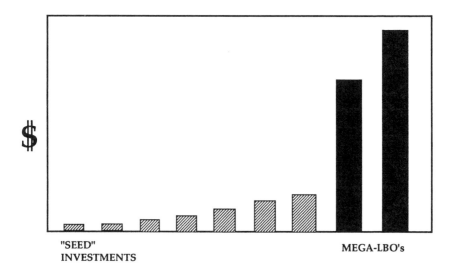

The figure above depicts the situation today that is commonly called the venture capital industry. The continuum runs from left to right. On the left there's real "seed capital" investing in brand new ventures. At the extreme right are "bankable deals." The entire area between gets inaccurately classified as VENTURE CAPITAL. Most of the money is in the far right portion of the range in the form of such things as mega-leveraged buy-outs like the RJR Nabisco deal. The RJR leveraged buy-out was the biggest sale of its kind. It took over $26 billion to complete the transaction. The company is just now starting the deleveraging process. It will take years to complete with very dubious benefit to the company. However, the deal makers made out fine.

Money in this area also comes from big venture capital groups to fund companies that they gave money to previously. Furthermore, Off-Balance-Sheet fundings, such as the selling of a company's headquarters building and then leasing it back to them, fall into this region of the continuum. Those sort of things are best described as "Investment Banking" or "Merchant Banking" activities. They are not really venture capital that will be of help to the typical entrepreneur.

While the estimates of the situation vary widely, less than 10% of the "formal" venture capital funds would even consider making investments in start-up or near start-up companies. Nevertheless, let's look at the Venture Capital Funds, because your deal is SO special. (The most complete directory to venture capital firms is the bible of the industry, *"Pratt's Guide to Venture Capital."*)

The first thing apparent in this search for funding is that the venture capital firms are concentrated on the East Coast, primarily in Boston and New York, and on the West Coast, primarily in San Francisco and Los Angeles. The few remaining organizations of consequence are in smaller markets.

What are the sizes of the funds? Venture Capital (VC) Funds are usually organized as limited partnerships to avoid the double taxation in a corporation. The partnerships or funds I consider the

"Big" ones have over $75 million. These funds remind me of the lunker trout I used to fish for in the wild streams of my home state of Idaho. Why? Well, the big trout would run off his lesser-sized competitors from the choice position behind a big rock in the stream. Here he was best situated to watch the food supply drift by him. He would lie there, with little or no effort, sheltered from the current by the rock. With one eye, he watched for especially good morsels of food. Such trout were hard to catch, because they were rarely hungry. After all, they had a moving smorgasbord of food passing by at all times.

The managers of a typical fund get from 2% to 3% of the total worth of the partnership's capital as their annual fee for running the business of the fund. They can fund a nice operational setting and a comfortable lifestyle without ever doing many deals. It is not surprising that the performance of these big funds has not been very good -- definitely less than the 35% compounded annual return they say is their target.

The "Little" funds are the ones with less than $10 million to invest. While $10 million is a lot of money, it really isn't for this industry. The managers try to provide themselves with some diversity. Yet, some under-performing investments (as there always are) and other real-life challenges, face the few partners who run such funds. They, like the entrepreneurs initially sponsored, wind up knocking on the doors of the big funds, insurance companies, and trusts to obtain additional funding for the few deals that are working out. Thus, the little funds become "finders" for the big funds. In return, the big funds become "money allocators" rather than venture capitalists.

Are there any real venture capitalists out there? There are a few, if you go along with my definition of a pure venture capitalist. Such a person or group should have a high degree of expertise and time devoted to "nurturing" small companies and furthermore, really enjoy the activity. I met such a person several years ago in Sacramento, California. His name is George Crandell. He'd been with one of the big VC firms but didn't personally enjoy the organizational setting. He preferred to be close to the entrepreneurs and their companies rather than run the fund's operations from the ivory towers. George and I met for breakfast because he didn't have a real office. He worked in a shared office location and only required the services such facilities provide. How could that be when he had the size of fund that would be classified as big?

He had a desk at each of the companies in which he had invested -- those companies that fit his investment criteria. In addition, they also had to meet his location criteria, which was to be within 90 minutes of his home in Sacramento. He's a guy who wants to be near his investments -- to help nurture each one as the situation warrants. He feels this is more productive than zipping all over the country, acting like a big wheel, and living off the expense account of some partnership's management fee.

Let's say you worked very hard on a proposal for a VC firm. You've used the best guide I've found for crafting such a document, David Gladstone's *"Venture Capital Handbook."* Your submission warranted an invitation to make an in-person presentation at the company. Your preparation has helped you understand how negotiations will go with the VC firm. They wouldn't have invited you to make a presentation if they didn't want to make a deal with you. So, how much should you be expected to give up of your enterprise for the money it will take to make it work?

Gladstone's book covers this subject very well as does another one called *"Entrepreneurial Finance"* by Robert Ronstadt. According to information gathered from these two authors, combined with my own experience, I feel it is best if the entrepreneur trades from 15%

to 30% of the company for the funding needed. If whoever puts up the money gets less than 15%, you won't be getting their close attention. In many cases, this is more important than the money itself. However, if the entrepreneur has to give up more than 30%, then the entrepreneur's motivation can drop off to the detriment of all concerned. The entrepreneur is the caretaker of the dream. Without having a major incentive to continue dreaming, the company and its shareholders will be hurt. Even with these loose parameters, the entrepreneur must use great care in the negotiation process. The venture capitalists will try to get whatever they believe you will agree to -- even if that means a majority interest in your company.

Entrepreneurs should understand that nobody, not even your mother, can be expected to put more than $1 million into an untried venture. With this in mind, any start-up or near start-up has to gear its presentation accordingly. Remember -- prove yourself first and the money will be there when you need it.

At this stage, it's best to put your emotions aside (i.e. -- Don't get hung up about words such as "control" and "power"). Check how good your proposition is by comparing it to other funded deals. Then decide what needs to be done to get you back into the acceptable range of 15% to 30%.

Use the following standards:

1. The percentage an investor obtains of an enterprise is directly related to how much he puts in. For example, the more he puts in, the more he gets.

2. The higher the investor's desired rate of return on his money, the larger his percentage of the company will be for the same amount of money invested.

3. **The higher the net profit generated by the enterprise, the more it is worth.**

The above elements are depicted mathematically as follows:

$$\frac{\text{Percent of}}{\text{Company}} = \frac{\text{Money Invested}}{\text{Net Earnings in Yr. 3}} \times \frac{\text{Target Rate of Return}}{\text{Appropriate P/E* Ratio}}$$

* Price of similar company's stock divided by its earnings.

Real Life Example:

$$27\% = \frac{\$1,000,000}{900,000} \times \frac{(1.35)^3}{10}$$

. . . where $(1.35)^3$ implies a 35% per year compound rate of return over three years.

While the use of three years is not hard and fast, less time doesn't fit with reality. A longer period is just too long a period to extrapolate anything even with the best of estimates.

The denominators of the two fractions, earnings multiplied by the price to earnings ratio, yields the worth of the company at the end of year three.

While the mathematics are important, it is infinitely more important you understand the relationships between the factors involved. For example, if by year three your enterprise has not made enough net profit, the investor would own most of the company if his rate of return criteria is met. You should play with each of the five factors in this equation until you thoroughly understand what happens as each is varied up and down. Ken Olson, the founder of Digital Equipment Company, has said that a CEO isn't really in charge of his business until he can spout from memory his balance sheet and profit and loss statement. In the same way, you're not really an entrepreneur until you can spout from memory how this equation applies to your enterprise.

For example, let's determine what it would take for the percentage of the company going to the investor to go down to 20% versus the 27% in the example above.

First, the amount of money invested could be decreased and the other factors kept at their same values. In that case, $731,707 would yield 20% of the company.

But what if $731,707 isn't enough to achieve lift-off of the enterprise? What if we reduced both the investors' rate of return goal to 30% compounded annually (1.30)3 together with an investment of $819,299? That gives us the amount we're seeking.

But what if the venture capitalist doesn't want to do any deals smaller than $1 million and is also firm on his rate of return goal? If you could do some things to earn a higher net profit in year three, how much would it have to be to yield the target of 20%? Answer, $1,230,000.

We could also have a discussion about what the P/E ratio would be if the three other original factors were left intact. 20% of the company would be achieved with a P/E of 13.7. Did you get that answer on your calculator? If not, try again.

So, what's the reality of working with a VC firm? Frankly, SLIM to NONE! However, don't despair. I will explain further in the following chapter the normal, expected way a venture capitalist can cash out of his investments by taking the investee company public. That's what this book is all about: Going public -- by yourself, slowly but surely.

RECOMMENDATION: DON'T GO TO VENTURE CAPITAL FIRMS
FOR YOUR FUNDING NEEDS.

6

WALL STREET
INITIAL PUBLIC OFFERINGS

▼

Initial Public Offerings (IPOs) are products distributed by investment bankers and venture capitalists. Local hardware stores sell for the lawnmower manufacturers. The shoe stores sell for the shoe manufacturers. In a similar fashion, the nation's major stock brokerage firms sell IPO's that are products put together in high-rise offices of Manhattan rather than lawnmower factories in North Carolina or in shoe factories in Missouri.

What is the cost of the "manufacturing process" to bring out a new issue of stock? It's very expensive. Normally, for issues of $20 million or more, the usual percentage for underwriting, organizing, and selling, is about 10% to 12%. Yes, $2 million! How else can the big investment banking firms pay such high rents and high salaries? On issues under $5 million, the underwriting fees run as high as 15% to 20%.

Wall Street used to be a more reasonable distribution system for the stocks of emerging companies. Now it's a gathering mechanism for collecting money to spread out with professional money managers. It's very difficult for most money managers to invest in small companies because of the relatively massive size of the funds they manage. Many run into billions of dollars.

From the accounting perspective, the big accounting firms have good books and pamphlets on the process of taking companies public.

RECOMMENDATION: FORGET ABOUT GOING PUBLIC IN THIS FASHION AT THIS TIME.

7

BLIND POOLS
AND PUBLIC SHELLS

I call this area of funding alternatives "The Entrepreneurs' Frustration Patch" and for good reason. I, too, have walked the halls of various office buildings of Southeast Denver looking for a way to raise capital using such methods. Denver became the capital for such activities. Why? Nobody is sure. It just happened, much to the dismay of both federal and state securities regulators.

Blind pool funding is a tactic where a company is created for the purpose of finding something to invest in at a later time. Some blind pools have enough money in them to make a significant investment, but most don't. The company has publicly traded stock, usually selling for less than $1 -- commonly called "penny stock" by the traders of such issues. Such trading is supposed to take place in response to the reputations of the blind pool founders for finding good investment opportunities.

Public shell funding is a technique where an existing company becomes essentially inactive and just waits around until a new company merges with it. There are shareholders who speculate that a new "hot concept" company will want to take this "backdoor" method of going public. They are generally penny stocks, also.

While the principles involved with these two methods of funding are not inherently bad, they have been the source of much abuse, such as brokers selling back and forth to themselves to create artificial activity in certain stocks.

RECOMMENDATION: STAY AWAY FROM OFF-THE-WALL APPROACHES!

SECTION SUMMARY

Except for the inherently high risks presented by blind pools, public shell funding, and the loss of relationships with family and friends, the various alternatives discussed in the section are not to be thought of as either "good" or "bad" -- at least in theory. However, from the two entrepreneurial examples given in the introduction to this book and from situations with which you are personally familiar, this list of alternatives falls far short of meeting the capital needs of the majority of small businesses in this country.

Don't despair! Help is on the way! It's been "coming" for over 10 years, but that's beside the point. Welcome the help that's finally here.

SECTION TWO

A Different Approach
to Capital Formation
for Small Business

With the demise of the Soviet Union, the various republics that have emerged are looking to the United States as the country they most admire and want to emulate. These people are asking for help in switching to a free market economy. They're looking for a model to follow. At the same time, we're in a massive reorganization and restructuring effort of our own economic system.

The SCOR process described in this section is intended by its originators to be part of the realignment of our business environment that will result in the development of viable mid-range businesses. Such businesses would have the potential to grow from $3 million in sales to $100 million and beyond. SCOR fundings can help accomplish that transition.

8

FUNDING ENTREPRENEURS IN A MARKET ECONOMY

▼

Now that we've discussed the various alternatives for funding entrepreneurial dreams, we'll cover a new funding approach involving the attainment of capital. Not just money -- capital!

Adequate capital is the key to business success. Why? Let's look at what happens without it.

If you ask a banker for a company that went bankrupt as to why it didn't survive, number one or two on his list of reasons would be, "They were under-capitalized." By saying that, the banker doesn't

---

mean that the company didn't have enough money. Money is not necessarily capital.

Capital is king! You don't have to pay pure capital back to anyone. Some form of loans are necessary for businesses to really grow, but should only be taken out after a solid base of real capital has been formed. As opposed to loans, however, capital doesn't require you to pay monthly interest for its use. Interest expenses keep piling up, day by day. No matter what, interest has to be paid regardless of the circumstances, good or bad, in business.

If capital is king, then flexibility is queen. Flexibility allows you to respond to the rapidly changing environment of today's business landscape. Capital provides for flexibility and, without flexibility, success for the company is seriously limited.

Can other entrepreneurs relate to your challenge? Absolutely! Some of their companies are now household names. However, they didn't start out big. They started small. Such companies as Hewlett-Packard, Federal Express, Nike, Apple Computer, McDonald's, and Wal-Mart are just a few of the companies that grew into mega-businesses because they were able to tap into the capital markets of this country's economy.

If you could, wouldn't it be great to reach into the capital markets like the companies above did? This book is all about how to do so. I feel that it is the best way for a small company to get the capital it needs to grow.

What and where are these capital markets we're talking about, and how do they relate to you, the entrepreneur?

Most people would say, "Oh, you're talking about the stock market!" They would be right, but there is a whole lot more to it than that. First, there is a market for stocks just as there is a market for vegetables, a market for clothes, or a market for auto parts. Next, there are various types of markets for stocks like there

---

are markets for food. Some are elaborate, some rather rough, and some are in between.

A market for stocks is where investing takes place. Investing should not be confused with saving. Investing by its very nature involves some degree of risk to the amount of money invested, normally called the principal. Inflation might be eating away at money in a savings account, but the principal amount is secure. This investing is done by individuals, banks, mutual funds and other such entities that have discretionary money they want to put at risk with the hope of future rewards. They want to purchase some of the potential of particular companies in specific industries they have deemed to be worth the risk of their funds.

What does an investor get for his money? In a word, stock. More particularly, a claim of partial ownership in the company that accepts the money. Such activity in our economy is covered on the financial pages of daily newspapers. In addition, you've probably viewed the activity of the national stock exchanges on the evening news on days with particularly noteworthy economic news.

What can happen when real capital is applied to a little business operating out of a garage? Hewlett-Packard and Apple Computer came from such a setting. Not every garage-based company has or will make it to the big time. However, it is my opinion that the SCOR process we're going to discuss will help a greater percentage do so than was possible in the past

In the same vein, not all of the 800 or so companies that are classified as Small Capital Issues being traded in the Over-The-Counter (OTC) market will ever make it to the OTC's National Market Listing or the New York Stock Exchange. Nevertheless, the stock of companies traded in this small company grouping must have $2 million in assets to be included. For a company to be a new addition to this category, it needs $4 million in assets. So, it all depends upon your definition of a small company.

What you as an entrepreneur should be stamping indelibly on your brain at this point is: "I can get all the money I need to grow my business!" The fact that you will most probably get that money incrementally, as you build your company and its track record of achievement, should not discourage you. As you and your associates prove you both need and can handle more money, it will be provided. The public has money to invest, especially on proven performers. You can go back to that well for more money -- capital, not loans, as many times as you are proven worthy of it!

That's the marvelous mechanism a market economy provides. Let's see how we can apply that capital funding method to your situation.

9

EVOLUTION OF THE
SCOR PROGRAM

▼

Governor Ronald Reagan had presided over California at a time of dynamic growth of small business. The phrase Silicon Valley was coined there. It came to stand for an environment where small companies rapidly evolved into large ones.

When he was elected president, one of the first things he did was call for a conference to stimulate small business. It was held in mid-1981 and was called the **White House Conference on Small Business.** This was the start of a new era for entrepreneurs in the

United States.

The conference attendees came up with a number of challenges plaguing small business. One of the those identified was:

> *It's hard for small companies to obtain investment*
> *capital from the general public.*

This wasn't a new revelation to any entrepreneur. Anyway, it was good to have it in writing. It started the process of trying to solve this vexing situation. The process involved assigning each of the problems identified at the conference to the government agency most directly involved with the situation. Someone within each agency's personnel became chairman of a task force to find a solution. Other governmental units involved, as well as professional and business attendee representatives, were assigned as members of each task force. The task force was to meet regularly and make recommendations to Congress and the executive branch. Specific recommendations were to be made for eventual elimination of each problem.

The task force involved with the investment capital issue was chaired by the U.S. Securities and Exchange Commission (SEC). It was called the **Government-Business Task Force on Small Business Capital Formation**. The members of the task force, along with other interested specialists (about 150 people in all) started meeting each year as a forum to work on this overall challenge and its associated sub-problems.

I've spent some time on various task forces to solve problems. In one case, it was to help resolve the problems of the C-5 Aircraft after Lockheed agreed to a $200 million loss in 1971. As task forces usually do, items are to be worked on in some fashion and a report made at each meeting. Each attendee is contacted by the chairman prior to the next meeting. He wants to know how the attendee is coming on his "action items." This causes an amazing thing to happen!

The membership in these ad hoc groups starts to mean a lot to the individuals involved. The loyalties developed are amazingly strong. You don't want to disappoint your fellow task force members. You start to really move and "do something." It is a prime example of how government can work within the proper framework.

The same thing began to happen in the SEC task force. The attendees from the American Bar Association (ABA), the American Institute of CPAs (AICPA) and others were assigned various "action items" at each of their meetings.

As the years went by, more evidence, both statistical and intuitive, was indicating that small business was the "Emerging Growth Engine" of the nation's economic future. Further encouraged, the members of the task force worked diligently on the overall problem. A master plan began to emerge. There was, indeed, a need and a reason to help create a fair and proper system for small public fundings. This was especially true when the penny stock market was causing so much havoc for the SEC in the early and mid '80s.

What eventually emerged was the desire for a funding process exempt from the high expenses of Wall Street IPO's. However, the private placement mechanism was already in existence. Why didn't small companies just use that? Simple -- it was too hard to get the amount of money needed. Plus, the investors have no ability to sell their stock, for any reason, even if they liked the proposal otherwise.

As the rough edges of the concept started to smooth out, the idea emerged of a simplified registration form. It could be a question and answer format. The entrepreneur, his regular corporate attorney (not an IPO specialist) and his regular CPA (not an IPO filing firm) could craft such a document. In turn, the various state securities personnel could review the document, both for completeness of disclosure and general business merit. As it stood before, all they received was notice from a company that it had done a private placement to sophisticated investors. As inducement for the filing of such an extensive disclosure document, the idea emerged to provide the shareholders with some degree of liquidity. Also, the prospective shareholders wouldn't have to be sophisticated investors. Neither federal or state securities regulators wanted to do anything that would in any way aid the trading in stock priced less than $1. Just a few cents' movement either way in such stocks could cause the large percentage moves leading to manipulation and abuse.

A compromise was eventually struck. It involved a methodology for a small company to sell up to $1 million in stock. However, the minimum price could not be less than $5 per share. Yes, that price was set arbitrarily. Nevertheless, the process can be very effective in this configuration.

With that settled, what was the filing document going to look like and who was going to develop it? The story began in Seattle, Washington, in the law firm of Bogle & Gates.

Mike Liles Jr. was an experienced securities law specialist at the law firm of Bogle & Gates in Seattle when his work began on the first SCOR (still called ULOR in Washington) documents. He worked with the Washington Securities Administrator, Ralph Smith, on these and the related regulations while serving on the Governor's Securities Advisory Board to the Washington Securities Division. The recession of 1981-82 created a strong desire in Ralph Smith to reduce the paperwork and hassle for small businesses in raising venture funds from the public.

At that time, there was a sense that small business, not big business, was the backbone of the U.S. economy. This predecessor was known as the Limited Offering Exemption, and the form, then called Form LOE-82, consisted of 25 questions for the applying entrepreneur. Liles used pre-existing questions already developed for clients who were attempting to assemble information to go public. The firm's experience with the use of these had been favorable, with some answers being so good that relatively few changes were needed in drafting a prospectus. This experience led to the use of the "question-and-answer" or "fill-in-the-blanks" disclosure document format for Form LOE-82.

In 1986, while serving on the State Regulation of Securities Committee of the American Bar Association, Liles was appointed to a study group chaired by Jean Harris of Phoenix, to assist as draftperson in designing SCOR and Form U-7. These documents would be used in state registrations for public offerings exempt from registration with the Securities and Exchange Commission (SEC). The group used Washington's Form LOE-82 as the model and expanded it to 50 questions. Additional advice for the financial statement requirements was sought and obtained from the Seattle offices of eight national and regional accounting firms.

SCOR was adopted by the ABA State Regulation of Securities Committee in 1987. In 1988, the Washington Securities Division was the first state securities regulator to adopt SCOR, and the North American Securities Administrators Association (NASAA) adopted SCOR in 1989. Today SCOR has been adopted by 25 states, and several others have it under active consideration.

The hard-working folks in Washington tried and tested the process and eventually rolled it out to the members of the task force at their 9th Annual Forum in Seattle in September of 1990.

Section Three

To SCOR or Not to SCOR?

The availability of a simplified disclosure document to allow a company to apply to securities regulators for authorizing a company to sell its stock to the public is one thing. The advisability of doing so is quite another matter.

In this section we will examine the SCOR process through the experiences of a hypothetical candidate company.

10

PROFILE OF A GOOD SCOR CANDIDATE

After reviewing the successful SCOR approvals in various states, a profile begins to form. The following characteristics, though generalizations, describe the ideal SCOR candidate company:

1. Existing Company
While start-ups can use the SCOR Program, an operational company with some type of track record is much more likely to

receive approval for the sale of stock in individual states. This is the necessary step that needs to be completed before selling your company's stock to the public.

2. Rapid Growth

The company's products and/or services are being well-received by the public. As orders increase steadily, the production capacity becomes increasingly strained to meet the present and perceived future needs.

3. Growth Industry

In order to generate the needed stock interest to the public, the company needs to have some investment "sizzle." To an investor, this could mean a number of things: innovative products or concepts, new technology or high tech processes. Whatever the situation, a solid perception must exist that the company's products or services have the potential to be a really big deal.

4. Solid Management Team

The basic management team, while probably stretched and in need of augmentation, is experienced in the industry. Additionally, there is a history of profitable operations under the current management. They meet established standards of honesty, social responsibility and competency. Looking at the growth of the company, combined with this experience, present management could be judged as being capable of running an expanding public company.

5. Lack of Capital

The company has probably run up against its line-of-credit limit at its bank, yet has orders or contracts that remain unfulfilled due to a lack of capital. The company can afford $25,000 to get the process started. Approximately $75,000 in additional progress payments for fees and expenses would be required in order to issue $1 million worth of stock over a 6-month period.

6. Existence of Natural Affinity Groups With Discretionary Cash to Risk for Long-Term Gain

For instance, a company produces solar-powered equipment. An affinity group to involve might be environmentalists. Plus, the company's existing customer base can hold considerable potential for stock purchases.

If your particular situation meets most of those characteristics, I'd suggest you take a closer look at SCOR.

PROFILE OF A GOOD
SCOR CANDIDATE

11

APPLYING SCOR
IN THE REAL WORLD

No matter what the nature of your business, it's necessary to properly organize your company to sell your products or services. There are rules and regulations associated with doing so, over and above whether there is a potential customer ready to buy your wares. Federal, state, and local laws dictate many things you must do to even start a business. Most likely, with this book in hand, you have those things behind you and are looking to expand your business. Nevertheless, you need to develop some sort of plan as to how you are going to grow it. Just hoping it happens isn't enough.

For discussion purposes, let's assume you have a new consumer product that appears to be a winner in some initial test marketing trials. Furthermore, let's assume you don't need additional funds to be able to make this new product. A reallocation of your present operating situation is all that is required. However, the new product is perceived to have a different "market" than your other products. You want to keep selling the old products still doing well. The goal is to replace the old products not doing well with the new product.

The challenge is to organize your company to sell your new product to the new market you have identified. No matter what you might call them, some sort of "meetings" or "discussions" are held to decide how you are going to approach this new market. You and your associates start with a few questions. In a short time, you expand to many more questions and some general agreement on an initial approach starts to emerge. New things will need to be done. They can cause a general trauma in any organization, let alone a small dynamic business such as yours. Nevertheless, you, being the good manager that you are, assign "the champion" of this new product the responsibility to develop an envisioned marketing plan along with the authority to draw upon the resources of the company for help. It is to be presented for formal consideration prior to implementation.

Let's say the champion and his team come back with a marketing plan and, with some minor modifications, it is accepted as what your company is going to do. Implementation then starts to shake the organization up because people tend to resist changes of any kind -- good or bad. Regardless, you as "the leader of the band" get out in front and sell this whole program throughout your organization. Why you? Because you're the chief executive officer and that's what's expected of you by your loyal partners, commonly known as employees.

Let's now jump ahead in this scenario to the point you and your key associates are meeting to discuss the success of your new product. Its success in early stages has been so good that it appears it could become a whole product line of merchandise. The topic of the meeting turns to, "Now what do we do?"

The first comment will most likely come from the person in charge of the company's cash flow, the chief financial officer (CFO) or the bookkeeper. It will probably go something like, "We need more money in this company to meet the production and sales you guys are talking about!"

This comment is not news to you because you and the CFO have been doing all you can to improve cash flow. You've been stretching out the accounts payable and accelerating the accounts receivable. Also, you've gone to your bank looking for an increase in your line-of-credit, but to no avail.

All eyes in the meeting turn to you. What are you going to do? This is the moment of truth for you and your company!

In business, there is no such thing as staying on a plateau at the present position. You're either growing or you're in decline. The loss of momentum is often ignored by the CEO. The first real sign of a loss of momentum is when the people who push for growth start to retreat from such activities and then start to leave the company. Sometimes the CEO has a feeling of relief when that happens because such people are always "stirring things up." It's much quieter without them around.

Let's say you feel your company can become a major enterprise in your region within the next few years. You've become a product of your past successes. Furthermore, you've done some research about obtaining capital by selling some of the stock of your company to the public. You even bought this book to further expand your knowledge on the subject. Thus, being armed with the information gained, you announce to your staff, "We're going to get a million dollars from the people of this area to expand our business!"

"How are we going to do that?" they ask.

"Just like we organized to sell our new product," you reply.

You explain that over the last few years various people have offered to buy stock in your fast-growing company, but they wanted control of it in exchange. You and your people haven't gone through all the growing pains with your company to become employees of a big company again. Consequently, you've turned such offers down. Yet, in looking at such demand, it appears there really is a market for the stock of your company. The task then is very similar to what your company just experienced in the process of planning for and implementing the roll-out of a new product line. Only this time the product is 8 1/2" X 11" pieces of paper. These stock certificates represent a claim, for example, of 1,000 shares of your company's stock. That in turn means that the holder of that piece of paper has a small portion of the 15% to 30% of the company you are planning to sell to the public.

The next comment might be, "But what do we know about selling stock? We're not stockbrokers!"

Your response might be: "Would you consider selling your house without the aid of a real estate agent?"

Upon getting a few affirmative nods you then say, "Well, it's a similar situation with selling the stock of our company without the help of a stock brokerage firm as an underwriter of our initial public offering."

Another objection might be, "But what are the ramifications of state and federal securities laws? Don't people get into trouble doing such things?"

You answer, "I've been working with our corporate attorney to assess the situation as it pertains to our particular circumstances. The initial feeling is that a new process called SCOR, Small Corporate Offering Registration, might just be right for what we need. We can raise up to $1 million through that program."

You lean back in your chair and start to pontificate as bosses do, saying, "I know this will mean a lot of extra work for everybody. However, as we've discussed many times before, we, the management of this company, own it, for better or for worse! It appears that we're on the threshold of the major expansion that we've all been striving toward. Yet without new capital, such accomplishments seem very remote."

Sensing your team needs some reassuring, you do so after you've studied and understand the following three questions:

What will it mean for you to be a public company?

As a SCOR company you won't have to make quarterly or annual reports to your stockholders. You'll be what's called a non-reporting company until you grow out of the small business classification.

How much is all this going to cost?

It depends, mostly upon how much of the work you can and want to do on the project. In gross terms, however, the best estimate I have in this newly-developing activity is that it should cost between 10 - 12% of the issue for a $1 million offering. It should run from about $100,000 to $120,000 -- TOTAL -- audits, legal opinions, the selling of the stock -- THE WORKS! That is much less than what such an offering would cost if, although unlikely, a major broker/dealer would even look at doing an offering for you in the first place.

Several points need to be made with respect to the above cost estimates. First, my recommended approach is to go for the $1 million offering for the reasons we'll soon discuss. However, there is no absolute requirement for that amount. If you and your advisors feel your company can better afford and handle a $500,000 offering, you can do so.

Next, the cost of a SCOR offering is directly related to how much you and your people can and are willing to do on the project. If at an early time you can embark upon a dedicated "clean-up" of your company's corporate records, you won't have to pay your lawyer to do so in a pressure-packed and costly environment that can exist just prior to filing the documents.

Finally, all costs of the SCOR process are negotiable as to price and terms. Rest assured that you do not have to write out a check for $100,000, even if you have it. Your capacity and experience as an entrepreneur may allow you to work out "deals" with your business contacts to bring the project costs down.

How long is the process going to take?

Experience with the SCOR program offers some idea as to the length of time a company can expect to spend on the two major parts of the process. Though generalized, these minimums and maximums provide good yardsticks for appropriating the hours needed to successfully execute an offering.

	Minimum	Maximum
Crafting and filing documents	3 months	5 months
Selling of offering	2 months	4 months
TOTAL TIME	5 months	9 months

12

OTHER
CONSIDERATIONS

Recently I met with key executives of a real-world company who were faced with some serious and pressing funding problems. The following chapter is a sample of the advice I presented to them. It is much like the advice that would be given to any company in a similar situation.

The dynamics of this whole funding process require you to build your presentation around asking for the maximum amount of money you can presently get from SCOR -- $1 million. The key point in doing so is the potential for enhanced liquidity for your stock. The ability to buy and sell the created security in a fair and honest environment was the main reason this process was started in the first place. By filing to obtain the $1 million maximum, a company will be eligible to trade on the OTC Bulletin Board. Furthermore, The Pacific Stock Exchange has requested permission from the SEC to list and trade Maximum-SCOR-Filing Companies at its facilities in Los Angeles and San Francisco. Such companies would trade there on a two-year probational basis. Your stock is like merchandise for the "supermarkets" called stock exchanges. No matter how good your product is, if you can't get "shelf space," you are not going to have it actively traded. In your case, you are looking for that important liquidity factor which comes from being on an exchange or part of the active OTC environment.

Going public is far from a one-time process. Consider the following phenomenon.

A well-established public company announces that it's going to make a "secondary offering" of its stock. That means the company is going to sell previously authorized but unsold stock to the public. The present shareholders will then have less of the company. Why? Well, if they owned 100% before the secondary offering, they would own some percentage less than 100% after it is sold to the public. This process is called "dilution" and it is neither inherently good or bad. It all depends upon how it is applied.

The securities regulators have to approve such secondary offerings to make sure the potential bad things, primarily involving any unfair treatment of the public shareholders in favor of the "insiders," is not allowed. Dilution is good when the company needs:

1. To obtain expansion funds that will allow the company to

acquire a complementary company.

2. To build more plants to expand a product that is experiencing high consumer acceptance.

3. To build more retail outlets of a successful trial concept store.

4. To exchange a relatively high interest-rate bond for equity.

5. To achieve some combination of the above.

Sometimes a secondary offering causes the stock to go down and sometimes to go up. It all depends upon the company itself and the perceptions of the investing public as to how such new money will be applied and management's ability to do so. If your company is going to be successful, you will need continual access to the capital markets. A company that has a good idea or product cannot usually generate enough cash flow to catch the opportunities in the fast-changing environment of today's business landscape. A good example of this can be read about in an article in the March 2, 1992, issue of *Forbes* concerning a company called The Body Shop International. The company did not have enough money to expand fast enough to freeze out its competition. From the market it created in natural ingredient cosmetics, the other big cosmetics companies moved in to fill the gap. Perhaps not going to the public for money was a well-considered choice Body Shop made purposely, but having the ability to "go back to the well," as prudently needed and required, is what being a public company means. If you bypass being accountable to the SEC and to public stockholders, you're still giving up something. You give up having the money to capture opportunities at critical times. It's a trade-off, as with most things in life.

Having too much money might be a problem if the recipient were one of the high-tech groups that have been tossed money by the venture capitalists wanting to fund the next "bombshell" concept in computers or bio-technology. Such "sure thing" or "new concept" investments in emerging industries periodically get a flood of money from investors who don't want to miss getting in on the ground floor of the deal. Remember -- you are trying to become a public company, with obligations to the "little people" who have invested $500 or so in your venture. If your temperament is to look out only for yourself, then stop reading this book immediately! Still with me? Then just go about building your plan around the $1 million. If you say you only need $750,000, then let it be the minimum amount. Work up some things you would like to do to give you some breathing room over and above that minimum where everything has to go right, yet seldom does.

Remember, the SCOR regulations allow a company to return to the public market a year after obtaining its first million dollars. Documents have to be updated, as do financial statements, in order to obtain the next million dollars.

13

WHAT IT MEANS
TO BE PUBLIC

One of my SCOR seminar attendees reported back to me with the following story:

He left the seminar all fired up with the idea of eventually doing a SCOR. Within the next few days he brought up the subject of "going public" with his accountant. Her reaction shocked him. She replied indignantly, "If you want to be a public company, then you'd better get another CPA!"

Why would an obviously well-informed professional person

have such a reaction? Because there are, indeed, many laws, regulations, and reporting requirements that govern the business life of what is called a "reporting company." The accountant knew that such companies have to file quarterly reports, annual reports, proxy statements, as well as supplemental reports for significant events concerning such companies.

The reason that regular public companies are required to make such extensive reports goes back to the great stock market crash of 1929. Manipulations of the stock of various companies were judged by Congress to be one of the most pressing problems. In response, Congress enacted laws in 1933 and 1934 that sought to make the dealings of companies that sold their shares to the public more open. Thus, it was hoped that dealings in such securities would be as fair and honest as possible. The law of 1933 dealt with the various aspects of the stocks and bonds themselves -- the pieces of paper. The law that followed in 1934 dealt with the exchanges -- the places where the shares were traded and the people who carried out the transactions.

The developers of the SCOR concept knew that the degree of information disclosure required of reporting companies was just too much for every small company. Instead, they allowed for businesses filing under the SCOR regulations to be non-reporting companies. In a nutshell, the SCOR filing companies need only keep minimal records such as current financial reports. Using only these reports, law requires that you distribute these to your investors for five years following the sale. The only time a SCOR company is required by law to report to their filing states is if materially detrimental things happen to the company. Otherwise, they simply run their businesses with the idea that they are responsible in every way to be honest and fair with all their shareholders.

After all is said and done, becoming a public company under the SCOR program does not impose any significant objectional reporting requirements.

SECTION SUMMARY

We'll leave our hypothetical company now. They will have to keep their company running while they embark upon the two major tasks associated with doing a SCOR.

First, the completing of the registration documents that will permit the selling of stock to the public (covered in Section Four), and second, organizing to sell the offering.

SECTION FOUR

Registering to Sell Your Company's Stock

We've covered a lot of information so far. We started by exploring the various alternatives to funding an entrepreneurial dream, along with the advantages and disadvantages of each.

Second, you were introduced to a new funding alternative called

Small Corporate Offering Registration, better known as SCOR. We discussed how this process fits into the country's market economy and capital formation activities. Then, in the last Section, we covered how SCOR could be applied to companies that fit a general suitability profile.

You are now ready to start working on the first task of doing a SCOR funding -- the completion of the disclosure document. The "U" designation developed in Washington state gives it proper status with the other "U" forms used in the securities industry.

14

THE BASIC PREMISE

If you are motivated enough to still be reading this book, you can fill out the basic form for the registration, the disclosure document known as Form U-7. Whether you want to do so after finishing the book is another question.

A key factor to keep in mind during the registration process is that the prepared document serves two purposes. It's the means by which you can pass the penetrating scrutiny of the securities regulators and it's the only sales tool you will be allowed to use to convince potential investors they should put their hard-earned money into your enterprise. Therefore, throughout the registration process, you will be required to walk a fine line between the blandness of a typical prospectus and the excitement of a sales brochure.

Is this process hard? Yes, it is! You need to ask yourself what are you willing to do and how hard are you willing to work to get the money to help fulfill your entrepreneurial dream. The mechanism is here. The question is, do you have what it takes to get the process completed? Sure you do! It just takes some hard work on those tough questions.

If your time is worth anything, this paragraph is worth the price you paid for this book! There is a special methodology involved when filling out forms for state governments, whether it's the U-7 or a form for an environmental project. The normal tendency for someone like myself who has written many business plans and funding proposals, is to read the particular question, get a feel for the general intent of what is wanted, and then set out to write a nice flowing narrative on what I feel is warranted and applicable. Nothing could be more wrong!

What is desired is for each question, sub-question, and sub-sub-question to be specifically answered, in order. This procedure cannot be overemphasized. Once you understand the methodology, you can handle the task. It will still be difficult, but much simpler this way. You can do it. Just keep at it. It'll be worth the effort.

Once you have put together a good document and have taken it to the state you've chosen, what happens next? You'll probably get a letter in the mail asking you to agree to an extension of time for the state to complete its review of your package past the 15 days, or whatever the particular state has set up. What this means is that, if you don't agree, then the answer to your request to sell stock in that state is NO! Not wanting that answer, you need to agree to the automatic extension of time.

What happens next? In a couple of more weeks you will get what's called a "Comments Letter." It will contain opinions from the regulators on a variety of areas. First, they will tell you whether your project can be done as a U-7 filing (blind pools, gold mining and oil drilling, for example, are not allowed). If it can, they will also include what they think about your proposal in general terms. You must remember these people are accustomed to receiving documents that are written by professionals in the field of prospectus writing. Make yours just as special even if you have to hire a technical writer to help you.

You handle the comments letter in the same fashion as the basic U-7 form itself -- question by question. The regulators will want you to do such things as add clarifications in some places, take some things out in other places, and redo some computations in still other places. All of this is just what it takes to get permission from the regulators to sell your company's stock in their state -- and that authorization does not come easily!

15

ADVICE BEFORE YOU
GET STARTED

▼

Don't get discouraged with this process. I recommend you make arrangements to get the Form U-7 into your word processing system. If you try to use a copy of the form, it won't work because you will have to continually "cut and paste" as changes are needed. The space provided on a copy of the form will not give you the exact amount of space you need to answer each question. Sometimes there will be too much and sometimes not enough. The regulators will often ask you to add or delete certain information from the document. In order to keep this process as easy as possible and as professional as needed for approval, the computer or word processor is the preferred choice.

All of the 50 individual questions on the Form U-7 are important or they wouldn't be there. However, Questions 2, 3, 4, 9 and 29 are the KEY QUESTIONS. The rest may require assistance from your attorney and accountant, being specific to your individual company's situation. They are quite straightforward, but still take dedicated work to fill them out correctly.

If you choose your words carefully, you will be allowed to tell your exciting story.

So, it's up to YOU, the entrepreneur, the keeper of the dream, the boss, the person who got this whole process started -- to do the tough 10% of the document. The other people can give you advice about how to make what you've written better once you have gotten the basics on paper, but it is my opinion that only YOU can do justice to these KEY QUESTIONS. Once again, it's not going to be easy, but if you can't or won't do it, it probably won't get done. With this in mind, we'll now cover each one of those key questions in detail.

Advice on Question #2:
RISK FACTORS

A bit of philosophy is needed at this point.

It has always seemed to me that the object of the "Statement of Risks" portion of any investment memorandum is to convince any prospective investors they would be crazy to even consider putting their money into a scheme such as this one -- especially with the particular people who are proposing to run such an enterprise!

Essentially, that is just who this question is for! To do otherwise would leave you open to not fully disclosing all the reasons this proposal might not work in spite of your total devotion to the goals of fulfilling your fondest dreams.

It is not the nature of someone like yourself to think about failing! Nevertheless, you must do so in order to protect yourself. Think of this question as your insurance policy section and do everything within your power to clearly outline the real risks pertaining to this venture.

The instructions say to be specific and not general. Regardless, I feel the examples of risks listed below are applicable to most immature business situations. You should then add others specific to your situation.

Limited Operating History. The company is in the early stages of operation. The operations of the company are subject to all the risks inherent in an immature business enterprise, including the absence of an extensive operating history.

Dilution. The current stockholders have acquired an interest in the company at an estimated cost per share substantially less than that which investors in this offering will pay for common stock. Therefore, an investment in the common stock offered will result in immediate and substantial dilution to investors.

Dependence on Key Personnel. In the conduct of the company's business, the company will be substantially dependent upon its present management personnel. The death or continuing disability of any of these persons may have a materially adverse effect upon the company's ability to conduct its business.

Absence of a Public Market. There is no established public market for the company's common stock and no assurance can be given that a public market for the common stock will ever develop. If such a market does develop, there is no guarantee it will be sustained. Therefore, purchasers may experience substantial difficulty in selling their shares of common stock should they desire to do so. Accordingly, an investor may not be able to liquidate an investment in the common stock quickly or on acceptable terms, if at all, and may be required to retain the common stock for an indefinite period of time.

Offering Price. The offering price of the stock of at least $5 per share has been arbitrarily set, and is not based upon earnings or any other historical operation. It should not be construed as indicative of present or anticipated future value of the common stock.

Limited Capital. Management of the company has made its best estimates of the minimum amount of capital needed to allow the company to achieve profitability in the first year.

Competition. The competitive environment has been assessed and evaluated by the management team of the company as it presently exists. No assurance can be given that competition from a new source or entity could not choose to enter this industry. Such entry could have a substantial impact on the future success and viability of the company making this offering.

Technology. The technology involved with the general business of the offering company is judged by its management to be in the forefront of the industry. Nevertheless, no assurance can be given that a technological break-through might occur causing the

---

described industry to be at risk of obsolescence, let alone the viability of this particular company.

A thorough review of the risk factors involved is the perfect "reality check" needed for the health of any company. These questions challenge you to face the true risks of your enterprise and hopefully defend against them as needed.

Advice on Question #3:
BUSINESS AND PROPERTIES

This question constitutes what would normally be considered as a "business plan" in its commonly used context. Unless you're very unusual, this question will throw you for a loop without following this advice. There are numerous "Business Plan Formats" available. The companion publications from Lord Publishing, *"Venture Feasibility Planning Guide -- Your First Step Before Writing a Business Plan"* and *"The Business Plan"* are the best I've seen. In any case, use a format other than the one laid out in this question, which is as follows:

a. The Company.

b. The Company's Planned Operations.

c. The Industry the Company is in.

d. The Company's Marketing Plan.

e. The Company's Backlog of Work.

f. The Company's Employees.

g. The Company's Tangible Property.

h. The Company's Intangible Property.

i. The Company's Regulatory Environment.

j. The Company's Subsidiaries.

k. The Company's History Over the Last Five Years.

Compare the above outline to whichever business plan model you choose. You'll find they vary greatly. My advice is to set the work on the SCOR filing aside for awhile and pour yourself into doing a business plan using whichever model you feel most comfortable with or seems to fit your company's situation best. You can then go back and work on Question #3 by plugging the appropriate answers into the appropriate spots, question by question.

The effort is worth it. This question alone will constitute from 35% to 45% of the total disclosure document and 80% of the information used to sell the offering. This is the only place that you can interest and excite the potential investor.

If you're not sold on the business and opportunity for profit, no one else is going to be. You can't "blue-sky" the opportunity, but you can polish and shine it. If the sale is not made here, it probably won't be made at all.

Advice on Question #4:
MILESTONES

This is a good exercise and is not part of most business plan formats. If you have ever been involved in a major project, you probably know the benefit of having a plan and working the plan. It is hard to envision how everything fits in time and operation unless you organize the project in some sort of visual presentation. I did my master's degree project on the construction of a major building. I had become familiar with Program Evaluation and Review Technique (PERT) and Critical Path Method (CPM) while serving as a systems development engineer in the military. Applying those techniques to the building project helped me to more fully understand how interdependent all the items of a project are and how vital it is to know the critical relationships.

My tutor on that project was a fellow officer, James E. Hines. He has a master's degree in architecture and a minor in urban planning. After his military service, he went on to do such projects as the 16th Street Walking Mall designed by the world renowned architect I.M. Pei in Denver, Colorado. We were recently together on that site. He explained to me that had they not used such planning techniques, the Mall probably would not have been completed at all, and if it had, it would have cost much more than planned. For instance, the trees landscaping the mall had to be ordered and planted at a nearby farm for two years so they could become acclimated to the mile-high altitude.

Your enterprise deserves this type of detailed planning. If you don't know how to do it yourself, then get help from someone who does. This is not a newly discovered requirement. From the Gospel of Luke (14:28) we read, "For which of you, intending to build a tower, sitteth not down first, and counteth the cost, whether he have sufficient to finish it?"

In essence, you must build your business on paper before you build it out of bricks and mortar. I'm continually amazed at how people are so anxious to DO something, even if it's wrong, rather than do the proper planning. Things are not always going to work out even with the best of plans, but you can be assured they won't work out if you don't plan properly. Life is complicated enough even when you do plan. My previous training taught me to always know where the nearest place was to land our aircraft. It's no less important for the navigating of your company from where it is now to where you want it to be.

As an exercise to get started, just pick some event, any proposed action in the future you are going to need this money from SCOR to accomplish. Then determine what needs to happen before that event and which things will happen after that event. Now, of the events before and the events after your chosen one, start placing them in rough order. You don't need to be precise at this point. Just get into the process. It's usually best to depict the events in some sort of boxes or circles as the relationships start to take shape. You will soon find that you need a big sheet of paper to have any feel for what you've done. If you will spend just two hours in this exercise, you will quickly see how much you need such planning, even if the SCOR documents didn't require this work.

I'm aware of various planning programs for today's computers. I have not used any of them enough to make a recommendation of one that you might use. If you know how to use one, fine. If you don't, I would say you would be better off to just work through the exercise manually with the help of someone who knows the basics of organized project planning. The principles are the same, whether it's a tower or a company -- it's just a series of events and how those events are tied together to accomplish a goal.

(See diagram on next page)

Advice on Question #9:
USE OF PROCEEDS

The previous key questions lead you to this one called "Use of Proceeds." In essence, what the securities regulators want to know on behalf of the potential investors in your company is: At what amount of money can your enterprise achieve enough power to reach sustained profitability and how will you spend the invested money to get to that condition? The assumption is anything less than that amount will not allow for sustained profitability, so if you can't sell enough stock in the maximum allowed period of time, then the money which has been held in escrow will be returned to the investors who sent it in to buy your stock. That's what the minimum scenario is all about.

The maximum funding under the SCOR program is $1 million. To cite another airplane analogy, the take-off calculations might indicate that the amount of runway required is 7,000 feet. Nevertheless, it's nice to have 10,000 feet of runway available, just in case one of the engines fails after the aircraft is committed to take-off. The same goes for some extra dollars over and above your estimated minimum.

Here's where the equation in Chapter 5 comes into play. If you have to give up more than 30% of the business to get up to $1 million of money invested, then you have to make some adjustments. Those adjustments to your situation will require that you reallocate funds

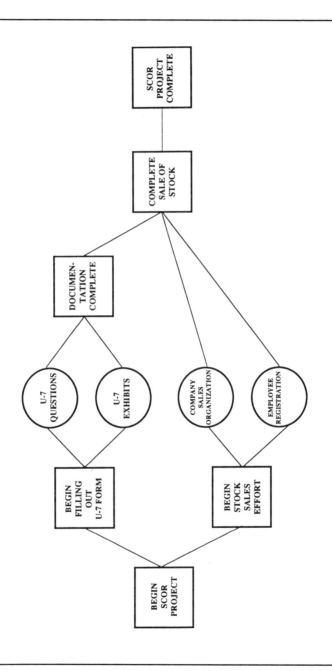

to, for example, improve the quality of your product so you will be more profitable and by so doing be able to justify that your company has a higher value. Sounds like a lot of work again, doesn't it? It is. However, the exercise in answering this question will allow you to know and understand your business in a way that you could not have imagined before undertaking the task of answering this question.

As a major hint as to how you can start the allocation of funds process, start with the number of "people" that you will need to run or expand your operation. My colleagues and I have found that once that is done, then everything else starts to take shape, for example, how big a facility you need to lease. Be as specific as possible.

Advice on Question #29:
OFFICERS AND KEY PERSONNEL

Let's talk about the "TEAM" you have assembled to help you run your enterprise. The best investors invest in "PEOPLE," not "THINGS." People will be the key to putting together your company. Put the team together first.

If you, by yourself, are the business, then you should stop everything until you've completed this crucial task. The people don't have to be working in the business right now, but you need to have them identified, positions for them chosen, salaries outlined. For all intents and purposes, you should be able to show what you will look like once the money from the investors comes to you.

Probably the most underrated position on the team is the position of Chief Financial Officer and the professional capacity of the person identified for that position. The securities regulators are "excellent numbers people." If you are not prepared with good financial data and with someone to help you with the financial task, then you are fighting an uphill battle to get through the registration process. For example, at a recent meeting of the UCLA chapter of the MIT - Venture Forum (a national organization of people interested in venture opportunities), three companies made presentations as part of their search for money. Each company's business plan was reviewed by a panel of experts prior to the meeting. While each company's presentation was well received by the audience, the panels did not recommend investing in the companies they reviewed. The main reason was each team didn't include a person with a strong financial background.

Once the team members are identified, then each of them has to go through the agony of putting together a narrative of their work experience. A typical resume format will not work for answering this question. It needs to be able to show expertise and accomplishments. You must do so in a straightforward manner. This question is one of the most difficult places in the document to walk the fine line between giving "just the facts" and "selling" the person.

The emphasis should be placed upon how the accomplishments covered in the work history of each team member supports the planned objectives of your company.

SAMPLE RESUME

Chief Financial Officer (CFO)

RESUME

Name: Richard Swift
Age: 38
Title: Treasurer and CFO
Office Street Address: 1234 Main Street
                               Anytown, USA   97654
Telephone: 314/555-1234

PAST EXPERIENCE:
(Names of employers, titles and dates of positions held during past five years with an indication of job responsibilities.)

Central Hospital
Vice President Finance, 1987 to Present

Arthur Anderson & Company.
Audit Manager, 1979 to 1987

Upon graduation, Mr. Swift was employed by the international accounting firm of Arthur Anderson & Co. in Anytown, USA. He joined the accounting and audit division and achieved the level of experienced audit manager. His clients included companies in a variety of fields including manufacturing, health care, grain export, barge companies and other service industries. His main responsibilities included the coordination and performance of audits and special projects with various clients. Mr. Swift developed a sound accounting and financial background during his nine years with Arthur Anderson with a solid understanding of the financial and accounting issues related to several industries.

Upon leaving public accounting in 1987, Mr. Swift was employed by Central Hospital, a 500-bed regionally recognized hospital. He was promoted to Vice President Finance with direct responsibility for 85 employees and all accounting areas. In addition to daily operating responsibilities he coordinated the financial feasibility studies on five major projects (totaling more than $15 million) and third party contracts comprising 20% of the hospital revenues (approximately $30 million). He also participated in several data system installations.

EDUCATION
(degrees, schools, and dates)

University of California,
BA Accounting (cum laude), 1976
University of California, MBA, 1978

Advice on Exhibits

The key factors pertaining to the following list of exhibits are that you will need to get the corporate minutes and other affairs of your company properly organized and updated. In addition, you will need to start the process of having your accountant do an official audit of your company's financial affairs. Furthermore, your attorney will have to prepare a formal legal opinion that your corporation has the ability and the authorization to issue the stock you are proposing to sell to the public.

The other items on this list of exhibits will be explained to you by your professional advisors. They'll be able to show you how each applies to you and your company.

Quoting from the U-7 instructions, "There shall be filed with the Administrator at the same time as the filing of the U-7 copies of each of the following documents to the extent applicable as exhibits to which the Administrator may refer in reviewing the U-7 and which will be available for public inspection by any person upon request."

In layman's terms, the following documents must be included in your filing.

Note: Exhibits preceded by an asterisk (*) have example documents attached at the end of this Section. All of the others will come from your company records or from your company's professional advisors.

1. *Form of Selling Agency Agreement (Form U-1).

2. Company's Articles of Incorporation or other Charter

---

documents and all amendments thereto.

3. Company's By-Laws, as amended to date.

4. Copy of any resolutions by directors setting forth terms and provisions of capital stock to be issued.

5. Any indenture, form of note, or other contractual provision containing terms of notes or other debt, or of options, warrants or rights to be offered.

6. *Specimen of security to be offered (including any legend restricting resale).

7. *Consent to service of process (Form U-2) accompanied by appropriate corporate resolution (Form U-2A).

8. *Copy of all advertising or other materials directed to or to be furnished investors in the offering (tombstone).

9. *Form of escrow agreement for escrow of proceeds.

10. Consent to inclusion in disclosure document of accountant's report.

11. Consent to inclusion in disclosure document of tax advisor's opinion or description of tax consequences.

12. Consent to inclusion in disclosure document of any evaluation of litigation or administrative action by counsel.

---

13. *Form of any Subscription Agreement for the purchase of securities in this offering.

14. Opinion of Counsel required in paragraph III.D. of these instructions.

15. Schedule of residence street addresses of Officers, Directors and principal stockholders.

ADVICE BEFORE YOU GET STARTED

16

FORM U-7 INSTRUCTIONS

The following are the "official instructions" on how to fill out Form U-7. The legalese will take some time to digest, but this will be the key to successfully completing Form U-7.

Don't be overwhelmed. Remember, doing a SCOR is not a weekend event. A good plan will take months of diligent work. I recommend skimming the information on your first read just to familiarize yourself with the scope of this process.

FORM U-7 INSTRUCTIONS

I. Introduction

Form U-7 has been developed pursuant to the Small Business Investment Incentive Act of 1980 (now contained in Section 19 of the Securities Act of 1933) which prescribes State and Federal cooperation in furtherance of the policies expressed in that Act of a substantial reduction in costs and paperwork to diminish the burden of raising investment capital, particularly by small business, and minimum interference with the business of capital formation.

Form U-7 is the greatest registration form for corporations registering under state securities laws securities that are exempt from registration with the Securities and Exchange Commission (the "SEC") under Rule 504 of Regulation D. It is designed to be used by Companies, attorneys and accountants who are not necessarily specialists in securities regulation.

Certain states in the registration of securities apply substantive fairness standards through various policies, rules and statutes. These standards, which vary from state to state, must be complied with by a company in order to register its securities in those states. Before using Form U-7, a company should discuss with the securities administrator of each state in which the offering is to be filed the application of substantive fairness standards to the offering.

II. Qualification for Use of Form

To be eligible to use Form U-7, a Company must comply with each of the following requirements.

A. The Company must be a corporation organized under the laws of one of the states or possessions of the United States which engages in or proposes to engage in a business other than petroleum exploration or production or mining or other extractive industries. "Blind pool" offerings and other offerings for which the specific business or properties cannot now be described are ineligible to use Form U-7.

B. The securities may be offered and sold only on behalf of the Company, and Form U-7 may not be used by any selling security-holder (including purchasing underwriters in a firm commitment underwriting) to register his securities for resale.

C. The offering price for common stock (and the exercise price, if the securities are options, warrants or rights for, and the conversion price if the securities are convertible into common stock) must be equal to or greater than $5.00 per share. By execution of the application and filing of the U-7 in any state, the Company thereby agrees with the Administrator that the Company will not split its common stock, or declare a stock dividend, for two years after effectiveness of the registration; provided, however, that in connection with a subsequent registered public offering, the Company may upon application and consent of the administrator take such action.

D. The Company may engage selling agents to sell the securities. Commission, fees, or other remuneration for soliciting any prospective purchaser in this state in connection with this offering may only be paid to persons who, if required to be registered, are appropriately registered in this state. It is a defense to a violation of this subsection if the Company sustains the burden of proof to establish that the Company did not know and in the exercise of reasonable care could not have known that the person who received a commission, fee or other remuneration was not, if required to be registered, appropriately registered in this state.

E. This form shall not be available for the securities of any Company if the Company or any of its Officers, Directors, 10% stockholders, promoters or any selling agents of the securities to be offered, or any officer, director or partner of such selling agent: (i) has filed a registration statement which is the subject of a currently effective registration stop order entered pursuant to any state's securities law within five years prior to the filing of the application for registration hereunder; (ii) has been convicted within five years prior to the filing of the application for registration hereunder of any felony or misdemeanor in connection with the offer, purchase or sale of any security or any felony involving fraud or deceit, including, but not limited to, forgery, embezzlement, obtaining money under false pretenses, larceny, or conspiracy to defraud; (iii) is currently subject to any state administrative enforcement order or judgment in which fraud or deceit, including but not limited to making untrue statements of material facts and omitting to state material facts, was found and the order or judgment was entered within five years prior to the filing of the application for registration hereunder; (iv) is subject to any state's administrative enforcement order or judgment which prohibits, denies, or revokes the use of any exemption from registration in connection with this offer, purchase, or sale of securities; (v) is currently subject to any order, judgment, or decree of any court of competent jurisdiction, permanently restraining or enjoining, or is subject to any order, judgment or decree of any court of competent jurisdiction, permanently restraining or enjoining, such party from engaging in or continuing any conduct or practice in connection with the purchase or sale of any security or involving the making of any false filing with the state entered within five years prior to the filing of the application for registration hereunder; (vi) the prohibitions of paragraphs (i) - (ii) and (v) above shall not apply if the person subject to the disqualification is duly licensed or registered to conduct securities related business in the state in which the administrative order or judgment was entered against such person or if the broker-dealer employing such party is licensed or registered in this state and the Form B-D filed with this state discloses the order, conviction, judgment, or decree relating to such person. No person disqualified under this subsection may act in a capacity other than that for which the person is licensed or registered; and (vii) any disqualification caused by this section is automatically waived if the state securities administrator or agency of the state which created the basis for disqualification determines upon a showing of good cause that it is not necessary under the circumstances that registration be denied.

If any of the circumstances in clauses (ii), (iii) or (v) of the preceding paragraph has occurred more than five years from the date of the application for registration hereunder, these circumstances should be described in response to Question 45 as a Miscellaneous Factor.

F. Use of the Form is available to any offering of securities by a Company, the aggregate offering price of which within or outside this state shall not exceed $1,000,000, less the aggregate offering price for all securities sold within the twelve months before the start of, and during the offering of, the securities under SEC Rule 504 in reliance on any exemption under section 3(b) of the Securities Act of 1933 or in violation of section 5(a) of that act. The Form is not available to a Company that is an investment company (including mutual funds) or is subject to the reporting requirements of paragraph 13 or paragraph 15(d) of the Securities Exchange Act of 1934.

G. The Company shall file with the SEC a Form D of Regulation D under the Securities Act of 1933 claiming exemption of the offering from registration under such act pursuant to Rule 504. A copy of the Form D with appropriate state signature pages shall be filed with the administrator at the same time as filed with the SEC.

III. General Requirements For Use of Form

A. The Form U-7 when properly filled in, signed and submitted, together with the exhibits scheduled below and a Form U-1 Uniform Application to Register Securities, constitutes an application for registration for the states listed at the bottom of the cover page of the Form. There should be filed with each state there listed a signed original of the Form, together with an executed Form U-1 and a signed original of the consent to service of process constituting Exhibit 7. Any references in the Form U-1 to SEC registration and effectiveness

---

should be disregarded and Questions 6 and 8(a) of
the Form U-1 are inapplicable. The Form U-1 should
set forth the amount of securities being registered
in that state and the method of calculating the
filing fee, and there should be enclosed a check
for the amount of the filing fee. Each state must
separately declare the registration effective by an
order to that effect unless that state has some
other procedure applicable to registration on Form
U-7. Once registration is effective as to a given
state, the effective date should be noted at the
bottom of the cover page of the Form. Any changed
or revised Disclosure Document must also be signed.

B. Each question in each paragraph of the Form
should be responded to. If the question or series
of questions is inapplicable, so indicate. Each
answer should be clearly and concisely stated in
the space provided; however, notwithstanding the
specificity of the questions, responses should not
involve nominal, immaterial or insignificant
information.

C. If the provided space is insufficient,
additional space should be created by cutting and
pasting the Form to add more lines or by putting
the Form on a word processor and adding more lines
in this or a similar manner. Irrespective of which
method is used, care should be taken to assure that
the Form is accurately and completely reproduced.
Smaller type size should not be used, and script or
italic type styles should be avoided.

D. There must be submitted to the administrator

---

an opinion of an attorney licensed to practice in a state or territory of the United States that the securities to be sold in the offering have been duly authorized and when issued upon payment of the offering price will be legally and validly issued, fully paid and nonassessable and binding on the Company in accordance with their terms.

E. The Disclosure Document on Form U-7 constitutes the offering circular or prospectus in a ULOR registration and the Form once filled out, filed and declared effective, may be reproduced by the Company by copy machine or otherwise for dissemination to potential investors. (The Company is cautioned to control the copying and distribution to preclude inaccurate or unreadable copies from being used and to prevent other unauthorized uses for which the Company may nevertheless be deemed responsible). These Instructions are not part of the Disclosure Document and should not be included. Reproduced copies should be on white paper and should be stapled or secured in the left margin without a cover of any type.

F. The Company should expect that the office of the administrator may have comments and questions concerning the answers set forth on the Form and that changes may be required to be made to the answers before the registration is declared effective. Comments and questions may either be included in a letter or made by telephone communication initiated by the office of the administrator in response to the filing.

G. No offers or sales may be made in this state until the registration has been declared effective by the administrator. To make offers or sales before the registration is effective could lead to a stop order or other proceeding which would preclude use of the Form in this or any other state and could give rise to a right of recession by investors enforceable against management, principal stockholders and the selling agents as well as the Company. When the registration has been declared effective in this state, offers and sales may be made in this state even though registration in other states has not been declared effective. This Disclosure Document must be delivered to each investor before the sale is made, e.g. (a) before any order is entered; (b) any subscription agreement is signed; or (c) any part of the purchase price is received. No registration statement shall remain effective for a period greater than one year.

H. After registration has been declared effective, and while the offering is still in progress, if any portion of the Form should need to be changed or revised because of a material event concerning the Company or the offering to make it accurate and complete, it shall be so changed, revised, or supplemented. If changed, revised or supplemented, (including an addition on the cover page of another state in which the offering has been registered) the Form as so changed, revised or supplemented, clearly marked to show changes from the previously filed version, should be filed before use with the administrator of this state. If any of the changes or revisions are of such significance that they are material to the making of an investment decision by an investor, and if the minimum proceeds have not been raised, after filing with and review by the administrator, the Disclosure Document on this Form as so changed, revised or supplemented should be recirculated to persons in this state who have previously subscribed, and they should be given the opportunity to rescind or reconfirm their investment.

I. Options, warrants and similar rights to purchase securities constitute a continuous offering of the underlying securities during the exercise period and require the securities to be registered and the Disclosure Document to be kept continuously current throughout the entire period. Upon any change, revision or supplement to the Disclosure Document, a copy must be promptly furnished to the holders of options, warrants and similar rights.

J. Any and all supplemental selling literature or advertisements announcing the offering should be filed by the Company and cleared with the securities administrator of each state prior to publication or circulation within that state. An announcement should not be a sales motivation device and should normally contain no more than the following: (1) the name of the Company, (2) characterization of the Company as indicated on the Cover Page of the Disclosure Document, (3) address and telephone number of the Company, (4) a brief indication in ten words or less of the Company's business or proposed business, (5) the number and type of securities offered and the offering price per security, (6) the name, address and telephone number of any selling agent authorized to sell the securities, (7) a statement that the announcement does not constitute an offer to sell or solicitation of an offer to purchase and that any such offer must be made by official Disclosure Document, (8) how a copy of the Disclosure Document may be obtained, and (9) the Company's corporate logo. Clip and return coupons requesting a copy of the Disclosure Document are permitted in printed announcements. (For example, an announcement in "tombstone" format with a black-lined border and using the following language would ordinarily be acceptable: *"50,000 shares, common stock; $5 per share; (Logo) XYZ Corporation, a development stage database computer software company now conducting operations; Midtown, Ohio; Selling agent: ABC Securities, 1234 Main Street, Midtown, Ohio, (321) 123-4567; This announcement does not constitute an offer to sell or the solicitation of an offer to buy the securities, which offer may be made only by means of an official Disclosure Document; a copy of the Disclosure Document may be obtained by* contacting the selling agent at the above address and telephone number. "

Similarly, a classified advertisement using the following language would ordinarily be acceptable: "Common stock of XYZ Corporation, a development stage database computer software company now conducting operations, Midtown, Ohio. Price $5 per share. Total offering 50,000 shares. This announcement does not constitute an offer to sell or the solicitation of an offer to buy the securities, which offer may be made only by means of an official Disclosure Document. A copy of the Disclosure Document may be obtained by contacting the XYZ Corporation, Industrial Park, Suite 12B, 456 Mill Road, Midtown, Ohio, (321) 321-4321. "

The issuance of any but routine press releases or the granting of interviews to news media during or at about the same time of an offering could constitute indirect advertising, which if not precleared with the securities administrator would be prohibited. Any unusual news article or news program featuring the Company during this period, particularly if present or future earnings, or the pending offering, are mentioned, could delay or cause suspension of the effectiveness of the registration and disrupt the offering. Consequently any such news article or news program, no matter by whom it may be initiated, should generally be discouraged during this period.

IV. Instructions as to Specific Captions and Questions

BE VERY CAREFUL AND PRECISE IN ANSWERING ALL QUESTIONS. GIVE FULL AND COMPLETE ANSWERS SO THAT THEY ARE NOT MISLEADING UNDER THE CIRCUMSTANCES INVOLVED. DO NOT DISCUSS ANY FUTURE PERFORMANCE OR OTHER ANTICIPATED EVENT UNLESS YOU HAVE A REASONABLE BASIS TO BELIEVE THAT IT WILL ACTUALLY OCCUR WITHIN THE FORESEEABLE FUTURE. IF ANY ANSWER REQUIRING SIGNIFICANT INFORMATION IS MATERIALLY INACCURATE, INCOMPLETE OR MISLEADING, THE COMPANY, ITS MANAGEMENT AND PRINCIPAL STOCKHOLDERS MAY HAVE LIABILITY TO INVESTORS. THE SELLING AGENTS SHOULD EXERCISE APPROPRIATE DILIGENCE TO DETERMINE THAT NO SUCH INACCURACY OR INCOMPLETENESS HAS OCCURRED, OR THEY ALSO MAY BE LIABLE.

A. Cover Page. The Cover Page of the Disclosure Document is a summary of certain essential information and should be kept on one page if at all possible. For purposes of characterizing the company on the cover page, the term "development stage" has the same meaning as that set forth in Statement of Financial Accounting Standards No. 7 (June 1, 1975).

B. Risk Factors. The Company should avoid generalized statements and include only those factors which are unique to the Company. No specific number of risk factors is required to be

---

identified. If more than eight significant risk factors exist, add additional lines and number as appropriate. Risk factors may be due to such matters as cash flow and liquidity problems, inexperience of management in managing a business in the particular industry, dependence of the Company on an unproven product, absence of an existing market for the product (even though management may believe a need exists), absence of an operating history of the Company, absence of profitable operations in recent periods, an erratic financial history, the financial position of the Company, the nature of the business in which the Company is engaged or proposes to engage, conflicts of interest with management, arbitrary establishment of offering price, reliance on the efforts of a single individual, or absence of a trading market if a trading market is not expected to develop. Cross references should be made to the Questions where details of the risks are described.

C. Business and Properties. The inquiries under Business and Properties elicit information concerning the nature of the business of the Company and its properties. Make clear what aspects of the business are presently in operation and what aspects are planned to be in operation in the future. The description of principal properties should provide information which will reasonably inform investors as to the suitability, adequacy, productive capacity and extent of

---

utilization of the facilities used in the enterprise. Detailed descriptions of the physical characteristics of the individual properties or legal descriptions by metes and bounds are not required and should not be given. As to Question 4, if more than five events or milestones exist, add additional lines as necessary.

D. Offering Price Factors. Financial information in response to Questions 5, 6 and 7 should be consistent with the Financial Statements.

E. Use of Proceeds. Use of net proceeds should be stated with a high degree of specificity. Suggested (but not mandatory) categories are: leases, rent, utilities, payroll (by position or type), purchase or lease of specific items of equipment or inventory, payment of notes, accounts payable, etc., marketing or advertising costs, taxes, consulting fees, permits, professional fees, insurance and supplies. Categories will vary depending on the Company's plans. Use of footnotes or other explanation is recommended where appropriate. Footnotes should be used to indicate those items of offering expenses that are estimates. Set forth in separate categories all payments which will be made immediately to the Company's executive officers, directors and promoters, indicating by footnote that these payments will be so made to such persons. If a substantial amount is allocated to working capital, set forth separate sub-categories for use of the funds in the Company's business.

If any substantial portion of the proceeds has not been allocated for particular purposes, a statement to that effect as one of the Use of Net Proceeds categories should be included together with a statement of the amount of proceeds not so allocated and a footnote explaining how the Company expects to employ such funds not so allocated.

F. Plan of Distribution. In Question 26, if the proposed business of the Company requires a minimum amount of proceeds to commence, or to proceed with, the business in the manner proposed, there shall be established an escrow with a bank or savings and loan association or other similar depository institution acting as independent escrow agent with which shall be immediately deposited all proceeds received from investors until the minimum amount of proceeds has been raised. Any failure to deposit funds promptly into the escrow shall be grounds for enforcement proceedings against the persons involved. The date at which the funds will be returned by the escrow agent if the minimum proceeds are not raised shall not be later than one year from the date of effectiveness of the registration in this state.

G. Capitalization. Capitalization should be shown as of a date no earlier than that of the most recent Financial Statements provided pursuant to Question 46. If the Company has mandatory redeemable preferred stock, include the amount thereof in "long-term debt" and so indicate by footnote to that category in the capitalization table.

H. Officers and Key Personnel of the Company. The term "Chief Executive Officer" means the officer of the Company who has been delegated final authority by the board of directors to direct all aspects of the Company's affairs. The term "Chief Operating Officer" means the officer in charge of the actual day-to-day operations of the Company's business. The term "Chief Financial Officer" means the officer having accounting skills who is primarily in charge of assuring that the Company's financial books and records are properly kept and maintained, and financial statements prepared.

The term "key personnel" means persons such as vice presidents, production manager, sales managers, or research scientists and similar persons, who are not included above, but who make or are expected to make significant contributions to the business of the Company, whether as employees, independent contractors, consultants or otherwise.

I. Principal Stockholders. If shares are held by family members, through corporations or partnerships, or otherwise in a manner that would allow a person to direct or control the voting of the shares, they should be included as being "beneficially owned." An explanation of these circumstances should be set forth in a footnote to the "Number of Shares Held."

J. Management Relationships, Transactions and Remuneration. For purposes of Question 39(b), a person directly or indirectly controls an entity if he is part of the group that directs or is able to direct the entity's activities or affairs. A person is presumptively a member of a control group if he is an officer, director, general partner, or trustee of beneficial owner of a 10% or greater interest in the entity. In Question 40, the term "Cash" should indicate salary, bonus, consulting fees, non-accountable expense accounts and the like. The column captioned "Other" should include the value of any options or securities given, any annuity, pension or retirement benefits, bonus or profit-sharing plans, and personal benefits (club memberships, company cars, insurance benefits not generally available to employees, etc.). The nature of these benefits should be explained in a footnote to this column.

K. Financial Statements. Attach to the Disclosure Document for the Company and its consolidated subsidiaries, a balance sheet as of the end of the most recent fiscal year. If the Company has been in existence for less than one fiscal year, attach a balance sheet as of the date within 135 days of the date of filing the registration statement. If the first effective date of state registration, as set forth on the Cover Page of this Disclosure Document, is within 45 days after the end of the Company's fiscal year and financial statements for the most recent fiscal year are unavailable, the balance sheet may be as of the end of the preceding fiscal year and there shall be included an additional balance sheet as of an interim date at least as current as the end of the Company's third fiscal quarter of the most recently completed fiscal year. Also attach, for the Company and its consolidated subsidiaries and for its predecessors, statements of income and cash flows for the last fiscal year preceding the date of the most recent balance sheet being attached, or such shorter period as the Company (including predecessors) has been in existence. In addition, for any interim period between the latest reviewed or audited balance sheet and the date of the most recent interim balance sheet being attached, provide statements of income and cash flows. Financial statements shall be prepared in accordance with generally accepted accounting principles. If the Company has not conducted significant operations, statements of receipts and disbursements shall be included in lieu of statements of income. Interim financial statements may be unaudited. All other financial statements shall be audited by independent certified public accountants; provided, however, that if each of the following four conditions are met, such independent certified public accountants in accordance with the Accounting and Review Service Standards promulgated by the American Institute of Certified Public Accountants: (a) the Company shall not have previously sold securities by means of an offering involving the general solicitation of prospective investors by means of advertising, mass mailings, public meetings, "cold call" telephone solicitation or any other method directed toward the public, (b) the Company has not been previously required under federal or state securities laws to provide audited financial statements in connection with any sale of its securities, (c) the aggregate amount of all previous sales of securities by the Company (exclusive of debt financing with banks and similar commercial lenders) shall not exceed $1,000,000 and (d) the amount of the present offering does not exceed $500,000.

If since the beginning of its last fiscal year, the Company has acquired another business, provide a pro forma combined balance sheet as of the end of the fiscal year, and a pro forma combined statement of income as if the acquisition had occurred at the beginning of the Company's last fiscal year, if any of the following exists: (a) the investments in and advances to the acquired business by the Company and its subsidiaries (other than the acquired business) exceeds 20% of the Company's assets on its consolidated balance sheet at the end of the Company's last fiscal year, (b) the Company's and its subsidiaries' (other than the acquired business) proportionate share of the total assets (after inter-company eliminations) of the acquired business exceeds 20% of the assets on the consolidated balance sheet, or (c) the Company's and its subsidiaries' (other than the acquired business) equity in income from continuing operations before income taxes, extraordinary items and cumulative effect of a change in accounting principle, if the acquired business exceeds 20% of such income of the Company and its consolidated subsidiaries for the Company's last fiscal year.

V. Exhibits

There shall be filed with the Administrator at the same time as the filing of the Form U-7 copies of each of the following documents to the extent applicable as exhibits to which the Administrator may refer in reviewing the Form U-7 and which will be available for public inspection by any person upon request.

1. **Form of Selling Agency Agreement.**

2. **Company's Articles of Incorporation or other Charter documents and all amendments**

thereto.

3. Company's By-Laws, as amended to date.

4. Copy of any resolutions by directors setting forth terms and provisions of capital stock to be issued.

5. Any indenture, form of note or other contractual provision containing terms of notes or other debt, or of options, warrants or rights to be offered.

6. Specimen of security to be offered (including any legend restricting resale).

7. Consent to service of process (Form U-2) accompanied by appropriate corporate resolution (Form U-2A).

8. Copy of all advertising or other materials directed to or to be furnished investors in the offering.

9. Form of escrow agreement for escrow of proceeds.

10. Consent to inclusion in disclosure document of Accountant's report.

11. Consent to inclusion in disclosure

description of tax consequences.

12. Consent to inclusion in disclosure document of any evaluation of litigation or administrative action by counsel.

13. Form of any Subscription Agreement for the purchase of securities in this offering.

14. Opinion of Counsel required in paragraph III.D. of these Instructions.

15. Schedule of residence street addresses of Officers, Directors and principal stockholders.

17

FORM U-7 AND EXHIBITS

Here is the Form U-7 in all its glory! This specific reprint should only be used as a reference to the information you will need when you actually begin filling out the real form. Nevertheless, you need to read through each question to get the flavor of what's being asked and why.

If you're going to do a SCOR, you will want to get the Form U-7 into your word processing system. Some states will provide a complete SCOR package. For $16 the state of Washington even provides you with a computer disk for your particular brand of computer.

In the following form and exhibits, [x] indicates that a written response is needed. In the same way, [$] would signify that a dollar amount is required.

FORM U-7

Exact name of Company as set forth in Articles of Incorporation or Charter: [x]

Type of securities offered: [x]

Maximum number of securities offered: [x]

Minimum number of securities offered: [x]

Price per security: [$]

Total proceeds: If maximum sold: [$]
If minimum sold: [$]
(For use of proceeds and offering expenses, see Question 9 and 10)

Is a commissioned selling agent selling the securities in this offering? [Yes or No]

If yes, what percentage is a commission price to public? [%]

Is there other compensation to selling agent(s)? [Yes or No]

Is there a finder's fee or similar payment to any person? **[Yes or No]** *(See Question No. 22)*

Is there an escrow of proceeds until minimum is obtained? **[Yes or No]** *(See Question No. 26)*

Is this offering limited to members of a special group, such as employees of the Company or individuals? **[Yes or No]** *(See Question No. 25)*

Is transfer of the securities restricted? **[Yes or No]** *(See Question No. 25)*

IN MAKING AN INVESTMENT DECISION INVESTORS MUST RELY ON THEIR OWN EXAMINATION OF THE PERSON OR ENTITY CREATING THE SECURITIES AND THE TERMS OF THE OFFERING, INCLUDING THE MERITS AND RISKS INVOLVED. THESE SECURITIES HAVE NOT BEEN RECOMMENDED BY ANY FEDERAL OR STATE SECURITIES COMMISSION OR REGULATORY AUTHORITY. FURTHERMORE, THE FOREGOING AUTHORITIES HAVE NOT CONFIRMED THE ACCURACY OR DETERMINED THE ADEQUACY OF THIS DOCUMENT. ANY REPRESENTATION TO THE CONTRARY IS A CRIMINAL OFFENSE.

This Company:

[ ] Has never conducted operations.
[ ] Is in the development stage.
[ ] Is currently conducting operations.

FORM U-7 AND EXHIBITS

[ ] Has shown a profit in the last fiscal year.

[ ] Other (Specify): **[x]**

(Check at least one, as appropriate)

SEE QUESTION NO. 2 FOR THE RISK FACTORS THAT MANAGEMENT BELIEVES PRESENT THE MOST SUBSTANTIAL RISKS TO AN INVESTOR IN THIS OFFERING.

This offering has been registered for offer and sale in the following states:

State File No.	Effective Date
[x]	**[x]**
[x]	**[x]**
[x]	**[x]**
[x]	**[x]**
[x]	**[x]**

INVESTMENT IN SMALL BUSINESS INVOLVES A HIGH DEGREE OF RISK, AND INVESTORS SHOULD NOT INVEST ANY FUNDS IN THIS OFFERING UNLESS THEY CAN AFFORD TO LOSE THEIR INVESTMENT IN ITS ENTIRETY.

TABLE OF CONTENTS

Section	Page #
The Company	**[#]**
Risk Factors	**[#]**

Business and Properties [#]

Offering Price Factors [#]

Use of Proceeds [#]

Capitalization [#]

Description of Securities [#]

Plan of Distribution [#]

Dividends, Distribution and Redemptions [#]

Officers and Key Personnel of the Company [#]

Directors of the Company [#]

Principal Stockholders [#]

Management Relationships, Transactions
and Remuneration [#]

Litigation [#]

Federal Tax Aspects [#]

Miscellaneous Factors [#]

Financial Statements [#]

Management's Discussion and Analysis
of Certain Relevant Factors   [#]

Signatures   [#]

THIS DISCLOSURE DOCUMENT CONTAINS ALL OF THE
REPRESENTATIONS BY THE COMPANY CONCERNING THIS
OFFERING, AND NO PERSON SHALL MAKE DIFFERENT OR
BROADER STATEMENTS THAN THOSE CONTAINED HEREIN.
INVESTORS ARE CAUTIONED NOT TO RELY UPON ANY
INFORMATION NOT EXPRESSLY SET FORTH IN THIS
DISCLOSURE DOCUMENT.

This Disclosure Document, together with
Financial Statements and other Attachments,
consists of a total of [#] pages.

THE COMPANY

1. Exact corporate name: [x]

State and date of incorporation: [x]

Street address of principal office: [x]

Company Telephone Number: [x]

Fiscal Year: [month/day - month/day]

Person(s) to contact at Company with respect to
offering: [x]

Telephone Number (if different from above): **[x]**

RISK FACTORS

2. List in the order of importance the factors which the Company considers to be the most substantial risks to an investor in this offering in view of all facts and circumstances or which otherwise make the offering one of high risk or speculative (i.e., those factors which constitute the greatest threat that the investment will be lost in whole or in part, or not provide an adequate return).

1: **[x]**
2: **[x]**
3: **[x]**
4: **[x]**
5: **[x]**
6: **[x]**
7: **[x]**
8: **[x]**

Note: In addition to the above risks, businesses are often subject to risks not foreseen or fully appreciated by management. In reviewing this Disclosure Document, potential investors should keep in mind other possible risks that could be important.

BUSINESS AND PROPERTIES

3. With respect to the business of the Company and its properties:

(a) Describe in detail what business the Company does and proposes to do, including what products or goods are or will be produced or services that are or will be rendered.

[x]

(b) Describe how these products or services are to be produced or rendered and how and when the Company intends to carry out its activities. If the Company plans to offer a new product(s), state the present stage of development, including whether or not a working prototype(s) is in existence. Indicate if completion of development of the product would require a material amount of the resources of the Company, and the estimated amount. If the Company is or is expected to be dependent upon one or a limited number of suppliers for essential raw materials, energy or other items, describe. Describe any major existing supply contracts.

[x]

(c) Describe the industry in which the Company is selling or expects to sell its products or services and, where applicable, any recognized trends within that industry. Describe that part of the industry and the geographic area in which the business competes or will compete. Indicate whether competition is or is expected to be by price, service or other basis. Indicate (by attached table if appropriate) the current or anticipated prices or price ranges for the Company's products or services, or the formula for determining prices, and how these prices compare with those of competitors' products or services, including a description of any variations in product or service features. Name the principal competitors that the Company has or expects to have in its area of competition. Indicate the relative size and financial and market strengths of the Company's competitors in the area of competition in which the Company is or will be operating. State why the Company believes that it can effectively compete with these and other companies in its area of competition.

[x]

Note: Because this Disclosure Document focuses primarily on details concerning the Company rather than the industry in which the Company operates or will operate, potential investors may wish to conduct their own separate investigation of the Company's industry to obtain broader insight in assessing the Company's prospects.

(d) Describe specifically the marketing strategies the Company is employing or will employ in penetrating its market or in developing a new market. Set forth in response to Question 4 below the timing and size of the results of this effort which will be necessary in order for the Company to be profitable. Indicate how and by whom its products or services are or will be marketed (such as by advertising, personal contact by sales representatives, etc.), how its marketing structure operates or will operate and the basis of its marketing approach, including any market studies. Name any customers that account for, or based upon existing orders will account for, a major portion (20% or more) of the Company's sales. Describe any major existing sales contracts.

[x]

(e) State the backlog of written firm orders for products and/or services as of a recent date (within the last 90 days) and compare it with the backlog of a year ago from that date.

As of   [date]   [$]
(a recent date)

As of   [date]   [$]
(one year earlier)

Explain the reason for significant variations between the two figures, if any. Indicate what types and amounts of orders are included in the backlog figures. State the size of typical orders. If the Company's sales are seasonal or cyclical, explain.

[x]

(f) State the number of the Company's present employees and the number of employees it anticipates it will have within the next 12 months. Also, indicate the number by type of employee (i.e., clerical, operations, administrative, etc.) the Company will use, whether or not any of them are subject to collective bargaining agreements, and the expiration date(s) of any collective bargaining agreement(s). If the Company's employees are on strike, or have been in the past three years, or are threatening to strike, describe the dispute. Indicate any supplemental benefits or incentive arrangements the Company has or will have with its employees.

[x]

(g) Describe generally the principal properties (such as real estate, plant and equipment, patents, etc.) that the Company owns, indicating also what properties it leases and a summary of the terms under those leases, including the amount of payments, expiration dates and the terms of any renewal options. Indicate what properties the Company intends to acquire in the immediate future, the cost of such acquisitions and the sources of financing it expects to use in obtaining these properties, whether by purchase, lease or otherwise.

[x]

(h) Indicate the extent to which the Company's operations depend or are expected to depend upon patents, copyrights, trade secrets, know-how or other proprietary information and the steps undertaken to secure and protect this intellectual property, including any use of confidentiality agreements, covenants-not-to-compete and the like. Summarize the principal terms and expiration dates of any significant license agreements. Indicate the amounts expended by the expiration dates of any significant license agreements. Indicate the amounts expended by the Company for research and development during the last fiscal year, the amount expected to be spent this year and what percentage of revenues research and development expenditures were for the last fiscal year.

[x]

(i) If the Company's business, products, or

properties are subject to material regulation (including environmental regulation) by federal, state, or local government agencies, indicate the nature and extent of regulation and its effects or potential effects upon the Company.

[x]

(j) State the name of any subsidiaries of the Company, their business purposes and ownership, and indicate which are included in the Financial Statements attached hereto. If not included, or if included but not consolidated, please explain.

[x]

(k) Summarize the material events in the development of the Company (including any material mergers or acquisitions) during the past five years, or for whatever lesser period the Company has been in existence. Discuss any pending or anticipated mergers, acquisitions, spin-offs or recapitalizations. If the Company has recently undergone a stock split, stock dividend or recapitalization in anticipation of this offering, describe (and adjust historical per share figures elsewhere in this Disclosure Document accordingly).

[x]

4. (a) If the Company was not profitable during its

last fiscal year, list below in chronological order the events which in management's opinion must or should occur or the milestones which in management's opinion the Company must or should reach in order for the Company to become profitable, and indicate the expected manner of occurrence or the expected method by which the Company will achieve the milestones.

Event or milestone	Expected manner of occurrence or method of achievement	Date, or number of months after receipt of proceeds when event should be accomplished
1: [x]		
2: [x]		
3: [x]		
4: [x]		
5: [x]		

(b) State the probable consequences to the Company of delays in achieving each of the events or milestones within the above time schedule, and particularly the effect of any delays upon the Company's liquidity in view of the Company's then anticipated level of operating costs. (See Question Nos. 11 and 12)

[x]

Note: After reviewing the nature and timing of each event or milestone, potential investors should reflect upon whether achievement of each within the estimated time frame is realistic. There is also a need to assess the consequences of delays or failure of achievement in making an investment decision.

OFFERING PRICE FACTORS

If the securities offered are common stock, or are exercisable for or are convertible into common stock, the following factors may be relevant to the price at which the securities are being offered.

5. What were net, after-tax earnings for the last fiscal year?

Total: [$]
(If losses, show in parentheses.)

Per share based upon number of shares outstanding after this offering if all securities sold: [$]

6. If the Company had profits, show offering price as a multiple of earnings. Adjust to reflect for any stock splits or recapitalizations, and use conversion or exercise price in lieu of offering price, if applicable.

Offering Price Per Share = [$] *(price/earnings multiple)* Net After-Tax Earnings Last Year Per Share

7. (a) What is the net tangible book value of the Company? (If deficit, show in parentheses.) For this purpose, net tangible book value means total assets (exclusive of copyrights, patents, goodwill, research and development costs and similar intangible items) minus total liabilities.

Price per share, based upon number of shares outstanding immediately prior to this offering:

[$]

If the net tangible book value per share is substantially less than this offering (or exercise or conversion) price per share, explain the reasons for the variation.

[x]

(b) State the dates on which the Company sold or otherwise issued securities during the last 12 months, the amount of such securities sold, the number of persons to whom they were sold, any relationship of such persons to the Company at the time of sale, the price at which they were sold and, if not sold for cash, a concise description of the consideration. (Exclude bank debt).

[x]

8. What percentage of the outstanding shares of the Company will the investors in this offering have? (Assume exercise of outstanding options, warrants or rights and conversion of convertible securities, if the respective exercise or conversion prices are at or less than the offering price. Also assume exercise of any options, warrants or rights and conversions of any convertible securities offered in this offering.)

If the maximum is sold: [%]
If the minimum is sold: [%]

(b) What post-offering value is management implicitly attributing to the entire Company by establishing the price per security set forth on the cover page (or exercise or conversion price if common stock is not offered)? (Total outstanding shares after offering times offering price, or exercise or conversion price if common stock is not offered).

If maximum is sold: [$]
If minimum is sold: [$]

(For above purposes, assume outstanding options are exercised in determining "shares" if the exercise prices are at or less than the offering price. All convertible securities, including outstanding convertible securities, shall be assumed converted and any options, warrants or rights in this offering shall be assumed exercised).

These values assume that the Company's capital structure would be changed to reflect any conversions of outstanding convertible securities and any use of outstanding securities as payment in the exercise of outstanding options, warrants or rights included in the calculation. The type and amount of convertible or other securities thus eliminated would be: [x]. These values also assume an increase in cash in the Company by the amount of any cash payments that would be made upon cash exercise of options, warrants or rights included in the calculations. The amount of such cash would be: [$].

Note: After reviewing the above, potential investors should consider whether or not the offering price (or exercise or conversion price, if applicable) for the securities is appropriate at the present stage of the Company's development.

9. The following table sets forth the use of the proceeds from this offering:

USE OF PROCEEDS

	If Minimum SOLD	If Maximum SOLD
	Amount/%	Amount/%
Total Proceeds	[$]/100%	[$]/100%
Less: Offering Expenses	[$]/[%]	[$]/[%]
Commissions and Finders Fees	[$]/[%]	[$]/[%]
Legal and Accounting	[$]/[%]	[$]/[%]
Copying and Advertising	[$]/[%]	[$]/[%]
Other (Specify): [x]	[$]/[%]	[$]/[%]

   (b) If there is no minimum amount of proceeds that must be raised before the Company may use the proceeds of the offering, describe the order or priority in which the proceeds set forth above in the column "If Maximum Sold" will be used.

[x]

Note: After reviewing the portion of the offering

---

allocated to the payment of offering expenses, and to the immediate payment to management and promoters of any fees, reimbursements, past salaries or similar payments, a potential investor should consider whether the remaining portion of his investment, which would be that part available for future development of the Company's business and operations, would be adequate.

10. (a) If material amounts of funds from sources other than this offering are to be used in conjunction with the proceeds from this offering, state the amounts and sources of such other funds, and whether funds are firm or contingent. If contingent, explain.

[x]

(b) If any material part of the proceeds is to be used to discharge indebtedness, describe the terms of such indebtedness, including interest rates. If the indebtedness to be discharged was incurred within the current or previous fiscal year, describe the use of the proceeds of such indebtedness.

[x]

(c) If any material amount of the proceeds is to be used to acquire assets, other than in the ordinary course of business, briefly describe and state the cost of the assets and other material terms of the acquisitions. If the assets are to be acquired from officers, directors, employees or principal stockholders of the Company or their associates, give the names of the persons from whom the assets are to be acquired and set forth the cost to the Company, the method followed in determining the cost, and any profit to such persons.

[x]

(d) If any amount of the proceeds is to be used to reimburse any officer, director, employee or stockholder for services already rendered, assets previously transferred, or monies loaned or advanced, or otherwise, explain:

[x]

11. Indicate whether the Company is having or anticipates having within the next 12 months any cash flow or liquidity problems and whether or not it is in default or in breach of any note, loan, lease or other indebtedness or financing arrangement requiring the Company to make payments. Indicate if a significant amount of the Company's trade payables have not been paid within the stated trade term. State whether the Company is subject to any unsatisfied judgments, liens or settlement obligations and the amounts thereof. Indicate the

Company's plans to resolve any such problems.

[x]

12. Indicate whether proceeds from this offering will satisfy the Company's cash requirements for the next 12 months, and whether it will be necessary to raise additional funds. State the source of additional funds, if known.

[x]

CAPITALIZATION

13. Indicate the capitalization of the Company as of the most recent balance sheet date (adjusted to reflect any subsequent stock splits, stock dividends, recapitalizations or refinancing) and as adjusted to reflect the sale of the minimum and maximum amount of securities in this offering and the use of the net proceeds therefrom:

Amount Outstanding

Debt:	As of: [date]	As Adjusted: Minimum/Maximum
Short-term debt (average interest rate [%])	[$]	[$]

Long-term debt
(average interest
rate [%])   [$]   [$]

Total debt   [$]   [$]

Stockholders equity (deficit):

Preferred stock -- par value times number of
outstanding shares (by class of preferred and in
order of preferences)

[x]   [$]   [$]   [$]
[x]   [$]   [$]   [$]
[x]   [$]   [$]   [$]

Common stock --
par value times number
of outstanding shares   [$]   [$]   [$]

Additional paid-in
capital   [$]   [$]   [$]

Retained earnings
(deficit)   [$]   [$]   [$]

Total stockholders
 equity (deficit)   [$]   [$]   [$]

Total capitalization   [$]   [$]   [$]

Number of preferred shares authorized to be outstanding:

Class of Preferred	Shares Authorized	Per Share
[x]	[#]	[$]
[x]	[#]	[$]
[x]	[#]	[$]

Number of common shares authorized: [#] shares. Par value per share, if any: [$]

DESCRIPTION OF SECURITIES

14. The securities being offered hereby are:

[ ] Common Stock
[ ] Preferred or Preference Stock
[ ] Notes or Debentures
[ ] Units of two or more types of securities, composed of: [x]
[ ] Other: [x]

15. These securities have:

[Yes or No] Cumulative voting rights
[Yes or No] Other special voting rights
[Yes or No] Preemptive rights to purchase in

new issues of shares
[Yes or No] Preference as to dividends or interest
[Yes or No] Preference upon liquidation
[Yes or No] Other special rights or preferences (specify): **[x]**

16. Are the securities convertible? **[Yes or No]**

If so, state conversion price or formula: **[$]**
Date when conversion becomes effective: **[date]**
Date when conversion expires: **[date]**

17. (a) If securities are notes or other types of debt securities:
1. What is the interest rate? **[%]**
If interest rate is variable or multiple rates, describe: **[x]**
2. What is the maturity date? **[date]**
If serial maturity dates, describe: **[x]**

3. Is there a mandatory sinking fund? **[Yes or No]**
Describe: **[x]**

4. Is there a trust indenture? **[Yes or No]**
Name, address and telephone number of Trustee: **[x]**

5. Are the securities callable or subject to

redemption? **[Yes or No]** Describe: **[x]**

6. Are the securities collateralized by real or personal property? **[Yes or No]** Describe: **[x]**

7. If these securities are subordinated in right of payment of interest or principal, explain the terms of such subordination.

[x]

How much currently outstanding indebtedness of the Company is senior to the securities in right of payment of interest or principal?

[$]

How much indebtedness shares in right of payment on an equivalent (pari passu) basis?

[$]

How much indebtedness is junior (subordinated) to the securities?

[$]

(b) If notes or other types of debt securities are being offered and the Company had earnings during its last fiscal year, show the ratio of earnings to fixed charges on an actual and pro forma basis for that fiscal year. "Earnings" means pretax income from continuing operations plus fixed charges and capitalized interest. "Fixed charges" means interest (including capitalized interest), amortization of debt discount, premium and expense, preferred stock dividend requirements of a majority owned subsidiary, and such portion of rental expense as can be demonstrated to be representative of the interest factor in the particular case. The pro forma ratio of earnings to fixed charges should include incremental interest expense as a result of the offering of the notes or other debt securities.

	Last Fiscal Year Actual	Pro Forma Minimum/Maximum	
"Earnings"= "Fixed Charges"	[$]	[$]	[$]
If no earnings, show "Fixed Charges" only	[$]	[$]	[$]

Note: Care should be exercised in interpreting the significance of the ratio of earnings to fixed charges as a measure of the "coverage" of debt service, as the existence of earnings does not necessarily mean that the Company's liquidity at any given time will permit payment of debt service requirements to be timely made. See Question Nos. 11 and 12. See also the Financial Statements and especially the Statement of Cash Flow.

18.   If securities are Preference or Preferred stock:
Are unpaid dividends cumulative? **[Yes or No]**
Are securities callable?   **[Yes or No]**   Explain:
[x]

Note: Attach to this Disclosure Document copies or a summary of the charter, by-laws or contractual provision or document that gives rise to the rights of holders of Preferred or Preference Stock, notes or other securities being offered.

19. If securities are capital stock of any type, indicate restrictions on dividends under loan or other financing arrangements or otherwise:

[x]

20. Current amount of assets available for payment of dividends (if deficit must be first made up, show deficit in parentheses):   **[$]**

PLAN OF DISTRIBUTION

21. The selling agents (that is, the persons selling the securities as agent for the Company for a commission or other compensation) in this offering are:
[x]

(include names, addresses and telephone numbers)

22. Describe any compensation to selling agents or finders, including cash, securities, contracts or other consideration, in addition to the cash commission set forth as a percent of the offering price on the cover page of this Disclosure Document. Also indicate whether the Company will indemnify the selling agents or finders against liabilities under the securities laws. ("Finders" are persons who, for compensation, act as intermediaries in obtaining selling agents or otherwise making introductions in furtherance of this offering.)

[x]

23. Describe any material relationships between any of the selling agents or finders and the Company or its management.

[x]

Note: After reviewing the amount of compensation to the selling agents or finders for selling the securities, and the nature of any relationship between the selling agents or finders and the Company, a potential investor should assess the extent to which it may be inappropriate to rely upon any recommendation by the selling agents or finders to buy the securities.

24. If this offering is not being made through selling agents, the names of persons at the Company through which this offering is made:

[x]

(include names, addresses, and telephone numbers)

25. If this offering is limited to a special group, such as employees of the Company, or is limited to a certain number of individuals (as required to qualify under Subchapter S of the Internal Revenue Code) or is subject to any other limitations, describe the limitations and any restrictions on resale that apply:

[x]

Will the certificates bear a legend notifying holders of such restrictions? **[Yes or No]**

26. (a) Name, address and telephone number of independent bank or savings and loan association or other similar depository institution acting as escrow agent if proceeds are escrowed until minimum proceeds are raised:

[x]

(b) Date at which funds will be returned by escrow agent if minimum proceeds are not raised:
[date]

Will interest on proceeds during escrow period be paid to investors? **[Yes or No]**

27. Explain the nature of any resale restrictions on presently outstanding shares, and when those restrictions will terminate, if this can be determined:

[x]

Note: Equity investors should be aware that unless the Company is able to complete a further public offering or the Company is able to be sold for cash or merged with a public company that their investment in the Company may be illiquid indefinitely.

DIVIDENDS, DISTRIBUTIONS AND REDEMPTIONS

28. If the Company has within the last five years paid dividends, made distributions upon its stock or redeemed any securities, explain how much and when:

[x]

OFFICERS AND KEY PERSONNEL OF THE COMPANY

29. Chief Executive Officer, Title, Name, Age, Office Street Address, and Telephone Number:

---

[x]

Names of employers, titles and dates of positions held during past five years with an indication of job responsibilities.

[x]

Education (degrees, schools, and dates):

[x]

Also a Director of the Company? **[Yes or No]**

Indicate amount of time to be spent on Company matters if less than full-time: **[x]**

30. Chief Operating Officer, Title, Name, Age, Office Street Address, and Telephone Number:

[x]

Name of employers, titles and dates of positions held during past five years with an indication of job responsibilities.

[x]

Education (degrees, schools, and dates):

[x]

Also a Director of the Company? **[Yes or No]**

Indicate amount of time to be spent on Company matters if less than full-time: **[x]**

31. Chief Financial Officer, Title, Name, Age, Office Street Address, and Telephone Number:

[x]

Name of employers, titles and dates of positions held during past five years with an indication of job responsibilities.

[x]

Education (degrees, schools, and dates):

[x]

Also a Director of the Company? **[Yes or No]**

Indicate amount of time to be spent on Company matters if less than full-time: **[x]**

32. Other Key Personnel:

Title, Name, Age, Office Street Address, and Telephone Number:

[x]

Name of employers, titles and dates of positions held during past five years with an indication of job responsibilities.

[x]

Education (degrees, schools, and dates):

[x]

Also a Director of the Company?   [Yes or No]

Indicate amount of time to be spent on Company matters if less than full-time: [x]

DIRECTORS OF THE COMPANY

33. Number of Directors: [#]   If Directors are not elected annually, or are elected under a voting trust or other arrangement, explain:

[x]

34. Information concerning outside or other Directors (i.e. those not described above):

(a) Title, Name, Age, Office Street Address, and Telephone Number:

[x]

Name of employers, titles and dates of positions held during past five years with an indication of job responsibilities.

[x]

Education (degrees, schools, and dates):   ·

[x]

Indicate amount of time to be spent on Company matters if less than full-time: [x]

35. (a) Have any of the Officers or Directors ever worked for or managed a company (including a separate subsidiary or division of a larger enterprise) in the same business as the Company?

[Yes or No] If no, explain: [x]

(b) If any of the Officers, Directors or other key personnel have ever worked for or managed a company in the same business or industry as the Company or in a related business or industry, describe what precautions have been taken to preclude claims by prior employers for conversion or theft of trade secrets, know-how or other proprietary information.

[x]

(c) If the Company has never conducted operations or is otherwise in the development stage, indicate whether any of the Officers or Directors has ever managed any other company in the start-up or development stage and describe the circumstances, including relevant dates.

[x]

(d) If any of the Company's key personnel are not employees but are consultants or other independent contractors, state the details of their engagement by the Company.

[x]

(e) If the Company has key man life insurance policies on any of its Officers, Directors or key personnel, explain, including the names of the persons insured, the amount of insurance, whether the insurance proceeds are payable to the Company and whether there are arrangements that require the proceeds to be used to redeem securities or pay benefits to the estate of the insured person or to a surviving spouse.

[x]

36. If a petition under the Bankruptcy Act or any State insolvency law was filed by or against the Company or its Officers, Directors or other key

personnel, or a receiver, fiscal agent or similar officer was appointed by a court for the business or property of any such persons, or any partnership in which any of such persons was general partner at or within the past five years, or any corporation or business association of which any such person was an executive officer at or within the past five years, set forth below the name of such persons, and the nature and date of such actions.

[x]

Note: After reviewing the information concerning the background of the Company's Officers, Directors and other key personnel, potential investors should consider whether or not these persons have adequate background and experience to develop and operate this Company and to make it successful. In this regard, the experience and ability of management are often considered the most significant factors in the success of a business.

PRINCIPAL STOCKHOLDERS

37. Principal owners of the Company (those who beneficially own directly or indirectly 10% or more of the common and preferred stock presently outstanding) starting with the largest common stockholder. Include separately all common stock issuable upon conversion of convertible securities (identifying them by asterisk) and show average

price per share as if conversion has occurred. Indicate by footnote if the price paid was for a consideration other than cash and the nature of any such consideration.

Name, office street address, telephone number, and principal occupation: **[x]**

Class of Shares	Average Price Per Share	# of Shares Now Held	% of Total	# of shares Held After Offering,if All Securities Sold	%of Total
[x]	[$]	[#]	[%]	[#]	[%]
[x]	[$]	[#]	[%]	[#]	[%]
[x]	[$]	[#]	[%]	[#]	[%]

Name, office street address, telephone number, and principal occupation: **[x]**

Class of Shares	Average Price Per Share	# of Shares Now Held	% of Total	# of shares Held After Offering,if All Securities Sold	%of Total
[x]	[$]	[#]	[%]	[#]	[%]
[x]	[$]	[#]	[%]	[#]	[%]
[x]	[$]	[#]	[%]	[#]	[%]

Name, office street address, telephone number, and principal occupation: **[x]**

Class of Shares	Average Price Per Share	# of Shares Now Held	% of Total	# of shares Held After Offering, if All Securities Sold	%of Total
[x]	**[$]**	**[#]**	**[%]**	**[#]**	**[%]**
[x]	**[$]**	**[#]**	**[%]**	**[#]**	**[%]**
[x]	**[$]**	**[#]**	**[%]**	**[#]**	**[%]**

38. Number of shares beneficially owned by Officers and Directors as a group:

Before offering: **[#]** shares (**[%]** of total outstanding)

After offering:
a) Assuming minimum securities sold: **[#]** shares (**[%]** of total outstanding)
b) Assuming maximum securities sold: **[#]** shares (**[%]** of total outstanding)

(Assume all options exercised and all convertible securities converted).

MANAGEMENT RELATIONSHIPS, TRANSACTIONS AND REMUNERATION

39. (a) If any of the Officers, Directors, key personnel or principal stockholders are related by

blood or marriage, please describe:

[x]

   (b) If the Company has made loans to or is doing
business with any of its Officers, Directors, key
personnel or 10% stockholders, or any of their
relatives (or any entity controlled directly or
indirectly by any of such persons) within the last
two years, or proposes to do so within the future,
explain. (This includes sales or lease of goods,
property or services to or from the Company,
employment or stock purchase contracts, etc.)
State the principal terms of any significant loans,
agreements, leases, financing or other
arrangements.

[x]

   (c) If any of the Company's Officers, Directors,
key personnel or 10% stockholders has guaranteed or
co-signed any of the Company's bank debt or other
obligations, including any indebtedness to be
retired from the proceeds of this offering, explain
and state the amounts involved.

[x]

   40.(a) List all remuneration by the Company to
Officers, Directors and key personnel for the last
fiscal year:

	Cash	Other
Chief Executive Officer:	[$]	[$]
Chief Operating Officer:	[$]	[$]
Chief Financial Officer:	[$]	[$]
Key Personnel: [x]	[$]	[$]
[x]	[$]	[$]
[x]	[$]	[$]
Others: [x]	[$]	[$]
[x]	[$]	[$]
Total:	[$]	[$]
Directors as a group ([#] of persons)	[$]	[$]

(b) If remuneration is expected to change or has been unpaid in prior years, explain:

[x]

(c) If any employment agreements exist or are contemplated, describe:

[x]

41. (a) Number of shares subject to issuance under presently outstanding stock purchase agreements, stock options, warrants or rights: [#] shares ([%] of total shares to be outstanding

after the completion of the offering if all securities sold, assuming exercise of options and conversion of convertible securities). Indicate which have been approved by shareholders. State the expiration dates, exercise prices and other basic terms for these securities:

[x]

(b) Number of common shares subject to issuance under existing stock purchase or option plans but not yet covered by outstanding purchase agreements, options or warrants: [#] shares.

(c) Describe the extent to which future stock purchase agreements, stock options, warrants or rights must be approved by shareholders.

[x]

42. If the business is highly dependent on the services of certain key personnel, describe any arrangements to assure that these persons will remain with the Company and not compete upon any termination:

[x]

Note: After reviewing the above, potential investors should consider whether or not the compensation to management and other key personnel, directly or indirectly, is reasonable in view of the present stage of the Company's development.

LITIGATION

43. Describe any past, pending or threatened litigation or administrative action which has had or may have a material effect upon the Company's business, financial condition, or operations, including any litigation or action involving the Company's Officers, Directors or other key personnel. State the names of the principal parties, the nature and current status of the matters, and amounts involved. Give an evaluation by management or counsel, to the extent feasible, of the merits of the proceedings or litigation and the potential impact on the Company's business, financial condition, or operations.

[x]

44. If the Company is an S corporation under the Internal Revenue Code of 1986, and it is anticipated that any significant tax benefits will be available to investors in this offering, indicate the nature and amount of such anticipated tax benefits and the material risks of their disallowance. Also, state the name, address and telephone number of any tax advisor who has passed upon these tax benefits. Attach any opinion or any

description of the tax consequences of an investment in the securities by the tax advisor.

[x]

Name of Tax Advisor, address, and telephone number:

[x]

Note: Potential investors are encouraged to have their own personal tax consultant contact the tax advisor to review details of the tax benefits and the extent that the benefits would be available and advantageous to the particular investor.

MISCELLANEOUS FACTORS

45. Describe any other material factors, either adverse or favorable, that will or could affect the Company or its business (for example, discuss any defaults under major contracts, any breach of by-law provisions, etc.) or which are necessary to make any other information in this Disclosure Document not misleading or incomplete.

[x]

46. Attach reviewed or audited financial statements for the last fiscal year and unaudited financial statements for any interim periods thereafter. If since the beginning of the last

fiscal year the Company has acquired another business the assets or net income of which were in excess of 20% of those for the Company, show pro forma combined financial statements as if the acquisition had occurred at the beginning of the Company's fiscal year.

The Company does hereby agree to provide to investors in this offering for five years (or such longer period as required by law) hereafter annual financial reports containing a balance sheet as of the end of the Company's fiscal year and a statement of income for said fiscal year, all prepared in accordance with generally accepted accounting principles and accompanied by an independent accountant's report. If the Company has more than 100 security holders at the end of the fiscal year, the financial statements shall be audited.

MANAGEMENT'S DISCUSSION AND ANALYSIS OF CERTAIN RELEVANT FACTORS

47. If the Company's financial statements show losses from operation, explain the causes underlying these losses and what steps the Company has taken or is taking to address these causes.

[x]

48. Describe any trends in the Company's historical operating results. Indicate any changes now occurring in the underlying economics of the industry or the Company's business which, in the opinion of Management, will have a significant impact (either favorable or adverse) upon the Company's results of operations within the next 12 months, and give a rough estimate of the probable extent of the impact, if possible.

[x]

49. If the Company sells a product or products and has had significant sales during its last fiscal year, state the existing gross margin (net sales less cost of such sales as presented in accordance with generally accepted accounting principles) as a percentage of sales for the last fiscal year: [%]. What is the anticipated gross margin for next year of operations? Approximately [%]. If this is expected to change, explain. Also, if reasonably current gross margin figures are available for the industry, indicate these figures and the source or sources from which they are obtained.

[x]

50. Foreign sales as a percent of total sales for last fiscal year: [%] . Domestic government sales as a percent of total domestic sales for last

fiscal year: [%] . Explain the nature of these sales, including any anticipated changes:

[x]
SIGNATURES:

A majority of the Directors and the Chief Executive and Financial Officers of the Company shall sign this Disclosure Document on behalf of the Company and by so doing thereby certify that each has made diligent efforts to verify the material accuracy and completeness of the information herein contained. By signing this Disclosure Document, the Chief Executive and Chief Financial Officers agree to make themselves, the company's books and records, copies of any contract, lease or other document referred to in the Disclosure Document, or any other material contract or lease (including stock options and employee benefit plans), except any proprietary or confidential portions thereof, and a set of the exhibits to this Disclosure Document, available to each investor prior to the time of investment, and to respond to questions and otherwise confirm the information contained herein prior to the making of any investment by such investor.

The Chief Financial Officer signing this form is hereby certifying that the financial statements submitted fairly state the Company's financial position and results of operations, or receipts and

FORM U-7 AND EXHIBITS

---

disbursements, as of the dates and period(s)
indicated, all in accordance with generally
accepted accounting principles consistently applied
(except as stated in the notes thereto) and (with
respect to year-end figures) including all
adjustments necessary for fair presentation under
the circumstances.

Chief Executive Officer:
Directors:

[signature]   [signature]
Title: [x]   [signature]
                                     [signature]

Chief Financial Officer:

[signature]   [signature]
Title: [x]   [signature]
                                     [signature]

FORM U-1

UNIFORM APPLICATION TO REGISTER SECURITIES

Application to [x] of the State of [x] pursuant to Section [x] of the [x]

1. Name and address of Issuer and principal office in his state:

[x]

2. Name, address, and telephone number of correspondent to whom notices and communications regarding this application may be sent:

[x]

3. Name and address of applicant:

[x]

4. Registration or acceptance for filing is sought for the following described securities in the amounts indicated:

[x]

5. Amount of filing and examination fees which are enclosed:

[$]

6. A Registration Statement was filed with the Securities and Exchange Commission on **[date]** and (became) (will become) effective on **[date]**.

7.(a) List the states in which it is proposed to offer the securities for sale to the public.

[x]

(b) List the states, if any, in which the securities are eligible for sale to the public.

[x]

(c) List the states, if any which have refused, by order or otherwise, to authorize sale of the securities to the public, or have revoked or suspended the right to sell the securities, or in which an application has been withdrawn.

[x]

Uniform Forms:

8. Submitted herewith as a part of this application are the following documents (documents on file may be incorporated by reference):

(a) One copy of the Registration Statement and

two copies of the Prospectus in the latest form on file under the Securities Act of 1933.

(b) Underwriting Agreement, Agreement among Underwriters, and Selected Dealers Agreement.

(c) Indenture.

(d) Issuer's charter or articles of incorporation as amended to date.

(e) Issuer's by-laws as amended to date.

(f) Signed copy of opinion of counsel filed with Registration Statement pursuant to the Securities Act of 1933.

(g) Specimen (type of security)

(h) Consent to service of process accompanied by appropriate corporate resolution.

(i) If an earnings computation or similar requirement is required to be met in this state, attach a separate sheet as an exhibit showing compliance.

(j) One copy of all advertising matter to be used in connection with the offering.

(k) Others (list each):

Form U-7 and Exhibits

9. The applicant hereby applies for registration or acceptance for filing of the above described securities under the law cited above and in consideration thereof agrees so long as the registration remains in effect that it will:

(a) Advise the above named state authority of any change prior to registration in this state in any of the information contained herein or in any of the documents submitted with or as part of this application.

(b) File with the above named state authority within two business days after filing with the Securities and Exchange Commission (i) any amendments other than delaying amendments to the federal registration statement, designating the changed, revised or added material or information by underlining the same; and (ii) the final prospectus, or any further amendments or supplements thereto.

(c) Notify the above named state authority within two business days (i) upon the receipt of any stop order, denial, order to show cause, suspension or revocation order, injunction or restraining order, or similar order entered or issued by any state or other regulatory authority or by any court, concerning the securities covered by this application or other securities of the issuer currently being offered to the public; and

(ii) upon the receipt of any notice of effectiveness of said registration by the Securities and Exchange Commission.

(d) Notify the above named state authority at least two business days prior to the effectiveness of said registration with the Securities and Exchange Commission of (i) any request by the issuer or applicant to any other state or regulatory authority for permission to withdraw any application to register the securities described herein; and (ii) a list of all states in which applications have been filed where the issuer or applicant has received notice from the state authority that the application does not comply with state requirements and cannot or does not intend to comply with such requirements.

(e) Furnish promptly all such additional information and documents in respect to the issuer or the securities covered by this application as may be requested by the above named state authority prior to registration or acceptance for filing.

Date: **[date]**
Name of Applicant: **[x]**
By: **[x]**
(Name and Title)

STATE OF **[x]**

COUNTY OF **[x]**

The undersigned, **[x]** , being first duly sworn, deposes and says:

That he has executed the foregoing application for and on behalf of the applicant named therein; that he is (title) of such applicant and is fully authorized to execute and file such application; that he is familiar with such application; and that to the best of his knowledge, information and belief the statements made in such application are true and the documents submitted therewith are true copies of the originals thereof.

Name: **[x]**

Subscribed and sworn to before me this **[day]** day of **[month]** , 19 **[year]**

NOTARY PUBLIC

In and for the County of **[x]**
State of **[x]**
My Commission Expires: **[date]**
(Notarial Seal)

SELLING AGENCY AGREEMENT

SELLING AGENCY AGREEMENT

Gentlemen:

ABC Company ("Company") is offering for sale 160,000 shares of Common Stock at $6.25 per share (the "Shares"), for an aggregate offering of $1,000,000, on a "best efforts, 120,000 shares-or one minimum, 160,000 shares maximum" basis. The Shares are offered through a Small Corporate Offering Registration (the "SCOR Offering), registered in certain states and exempt from federal registration pursuant to the Securities Act of 1933, as amended (the "33 Act"), Section 3(B) and Rule 504. The SCOR Offering is more fully described in a Disclosure Document which will be delivered under separate cover and the delivery of which you will have to acknowledge in writing.

1. Offering to Dealers.

RRMC is offering to certain selected dealers (the "Selected Dealers"), who are members in good standing of the National Association of Securities Dealers, Inc. (the "NASD"), subject to the terms and conditions hereof, the rights as set forth herein to sell a portion of the Shares to the public at the public offering price of $6.25 per Share. The Selected Dealers have agreed to comply with the provisions of Section 24 of Article III of the Rules of Fair Practice of the NASD. The Shares will be offered by Selected Dealers at the offering price. The Selected Dealers shall earn a commission of fifteen percent (15%) on Shares sold by each (the "Commission"), subject to the terms and conditions set forth herein and in the Disclosure Document. If you desire to offer for sale any of the Shares, your application should reach us promptly by telephone, telegraph or facsimile transmission at 9840 West Main Street, Belleville, Illinois 62202, (618) 394-0590. RRMC reserves the right to reject subscriptions in whole or in part, to make allotments and to close the subscription books at any time without notice. In purchasing, you will rely upon no statement whatsoever, written or oral, other than statements in the Disclosure Document.

Neither you nor any other person is or has been authorized to give any information or to make any representation in connection with the sale of the Shares, other than as contained in the Disclosure Document.

2. Escrow of Proceeds during Minimum Offering Period.

The proceeds from the sale of the 120,000 Shares-or none minimum offering will be placed in escrow with LOCAL BANK, West Main Street, Belleville, Illinois 62223, as escrow agent. In the event that a minimum of 120,000 Shares are not

sold during the one hundred eighty (180) calendar
day period commencing upon the effective date of
the aforementioned SCOR Offering (unless extended
up to an additional ninety (90) calendar days at
the option of the Company, the offering will be
withdrawn and the proceeds will be returned to
subscribers without interest and without deduction
for commissions or expenses. Such one hundred
eighty (180) day period, or such two hundred
seventy (270) day period, if extended by the
Company, is hereinafter referred to as the "Minimum
Offering Period."

3. Maximum Offering Period.

The proceeds from the sale of the remaining
150,000 Shares (Maximum Offering) will be paid
directly to the Company during the Maximum Offering
Period which shall commence with the Minimum
Closing Date and terminate three hundred thirty
five (335) calendar days following the effective
date of the aforementioned SCOR Offering
(hereinafter defined as the "Maximum Closing
Date").

4. Offering to Public.

You agree to make a bona fide offering of all
Shares allotted to you, and you will not offer to
sell any such Shares below the public offering
price of $6.25 per Share before the termination of
this Agreement.

5. Compliance with Securities Laws.

On becoming a Selected Dealer and in offering and selling the Shares, you agree to comply with all applicable requirements of the Securities Act of 1933, as amended, and the Securities Exchange Act of 1934, as amended. Upon application, you will be informed as to the jurisdictions in which the Shares have been qualified for sale under the respective securities or blue sky laws of such jurisdictions.

6. Subscribers' Payments.

During Minimum Offering Period payments will be placed in Escrow. Payments received by you for Shares sold during the Minimum Offering Period shall be made payable to LOCAL BANK, Escrow Account, and delivered to said bank, as escrow agent, by twelve o'clock noon of the next business day following receipt at the full public offering price of $6.25 per Unit, together with the name, address, social security or employer identification number, and number of Shares purchased by each subscriber.

During the Maximum Offering Period, payments received by you for Shares sold during the Maximum Offering Period shall be made payable to ABC Company. The above payment shall be made at the offering price or, if we so advise you, at a net price equal to the offering price less the Commission. If payment is made at the offering price, the Commission payable to you hereunder shall be promptly paid after payment has cleared at RRMC's bank.

7. Delivery of Shares.

Minimum Offering Period: A closing shall be held at the offices of LOCAL BANK or such other place as the Company may determine, as soon as practicable after the termination of the Minimum Closing Date. Certificates for the Shares sold by you shall be delivered to you in such names and denominations as you shall have requested, not later than three (3) full business days subsequent to the Minimum Closing Date and your selling commissions shall be paid to you promptly thereafter.

Maximum Offering Period: Certificates for the Shares sold by you shall be delivered to you in such names and denominations as you shall have requested, as soon as practicable following receipt and bank clearance of payment therefor.

8. Unsold Allotment.

You agree, upon our request, at any time, or from time to time, prior to the termination of this Agreement, to report to us concerning the number of Shares allotted to you pursuant to the terms hereof, which then remain unsold and to release to us, all or any portion of such unsold Shares as we may designate. In our discretion, we shall thereupon either offer all or any portion of such unsold Shares for sale to the public through other

FORM U-7 AND EXHIBITS

Selected Dealers, without obligation to you.

9. Reports of Sales.
You agree that any time, or from time to time,
at our request, to provide us with the names,
addresses and telephone numbers (if known) of, and
the number of Shares subscribed for by, each
subscriber of Shares and each person for whose
account Shares are subscribed or who has any
beneficial interest therein.

10. Position of Dealers.
You represent and warrant that you are a member
in good standing of the NASD and further represent
and warrant that you presently comply, and at all
times will comply, with all of the applicable
requirements of the '33 Act and the Securities
Exchange Act of 1934, as amended (the "34 Act"),
and with the Securities and Exchange Commission's
net capital Rule 15c3-1. You agree to comply with
the provisions of the Rules of Fair Practice of the
NASD, and, in particular Sections 8, 24, 25, and 36
of Article III of such Rules of Fair Practice. You
confirm that you are familiar with the rules and
requirements relating to a Small Corporate Offering
Registration and will comply therewith, as such
rules and requirements relate to you. RRMC will
make available to you such number of copies of the
Disclosure Document as you may reasonably request.
You will be informed as to the states and other
jurisdictions in which RRMC has been advised that

210

the Shares are qualified for sale under the respective securities or blue sky laws of such states and other jurisdictions and you represent and warrant that you will sell the Shares only in such states and other jurisdictions, but RRMC does not assume any responsibility or obligation as to the right of any Dealer to sell the Shares in any state or other jurisdictions or as to the eligibility of the Shares for sale therein. You represent and warrant that you have, or will, comply with all applicable laws, regulations and rules for selling the Shares in any states or other jurisdictions.

Nothing will constitute the Dealers an association or other separate entity or partners with RRMC or with each other. RRMC shall be under no liability to you, except for obligations expressly assumed in this Agreement and liabilities under the '33 Act, but no obligations on the part of RRMC shall be implied or inferred herefrom. The foregoing shall not be deemed a waiver of any liability imposed under the '33 Act.

11. Notices.

All communications to RRMC from you shall be addressed to RRMC, 9840 West Main Street, Belleville, Illinois 62202. Any notice from RRMC to you shall be mailed to the address to which this letter is mailed. Notices shall be deemed to complete on the third day after mailing.

12. Governing Law.

This Agreement shall be governed by and in accordance with the laws of the State of Illinois.

13. Termination.

This Agreement shall terminate on the Maximum Closing Date as defined in Section 3 and may be terminated by the Company at any time prior thereto. Such termination shall not, however, affect your obligation to pay for any Shares purchased by you or any of the provisions of Section 11 herein.

The SCOR Offering provides that unless at least 120,000 of the Shares offered thereunder are sold during the Minimum Offering Period, the offering will be canceled. Until the Minimum Closing Date or cancelation of this offering, all payments received from subscribers for the minimum 120,000 Shares will be held in escrow by Local Bank and if the offering is canceled, this Agreement will terminate and all sales by you and for your account hereunder will be similarly canceled, and all payments received will be refunded directly to the subscribers by the escrow agent without interest and without deduction for commissions or expenses.

Please confirm the foregoing and indicate the number of Shares you desire allotted to you by telegraphing your acceptance and order and by signing the duplicate copy of this Agreement enclosed herewith and returning it to RRMC at the address in Section 11.

Very truly yours,

ABC COMPANY

By: **[Signature]**
      Authorized Officer

We accept your offer to become a Selected Dealer on the terms specified above and acknowledge receipt of the Disclosure Document. In becoming a Selected Dealer, we have relied solely on the Disclosure Document and no other statements, written or oral.

On the terms set forth above, we hereby subscribe for an allotment of **[#]** Shares.

Address: **[x]**
Telephone: **[x]**
Identification Number: **[x]**

EXAMPLE OF STOCK CERTIFICATE

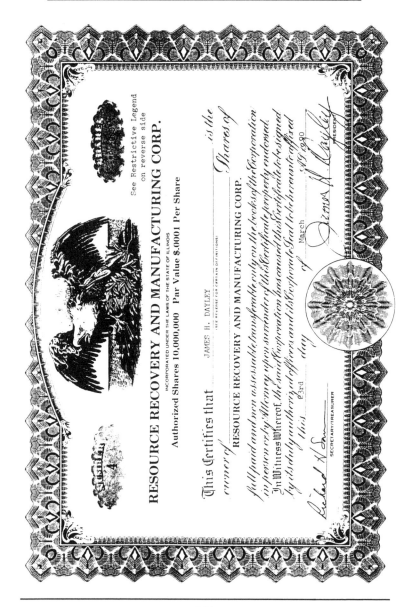

FORM U-2

UNIFORM CONSENT TO SERVICE OF PROCESS

KNOW ALL MEN BY THESE PRESENT:

That the undersigned, **[x]** (a corporation organized under the laws of the State of **[x]**) (a partnership) (an individual) (other **[x]**) for the purpose of complying with the laws of the **[x]** relating to either the registration or sale of securities, hereby irrevocably appoints the Secretary of State and the successors in such office, its attorney in the State of **[x]** upon whom may be served any notice, process or pleading in any action or proceeding against it arising out of or in connection with the sale of securities or out of violation of the aforesaid laws of said State; and the undersigned does hereby consent that any such action or proceeding against it may be commenced in any court of competent jurisdiction and proper venue within said State by service of process upon said officer with the same effect as if the undersigned was organized or created under the laws of said State and had lawfully been served with process in said State.

It is requested that a copy of any notice, process or pleading served hereunder be mailed to:

[x]

Dated: **[x]**   Dated: **[x]**
By: **[x]**   By: **[x]**
Title: **[x]**   Title: **[x]**

FORM U-2A

UNIFORM CONSENT TO SERVICE OF PROCESS

KNOW ALL MEN BY THESE PRESENT:

That the undersigned, ABC Company, a corporation organized under the laws of the State of Illinois, for the purpose of complying with the laws of the State of Washington relating to either the registration or sale of securities, hereby irrevocably appoints Securities Commissioner of the State of Washington, and the successors in such office, its attorney in the State of Washington upon whom may be served any notice, process or pleading in any action or proceeding against it arising out of or in connection with the sale of securities or out of violation of the aforesaid laws of said State; and the undersigned does hereby consent that any such action or proceeding against it may be commenced in any court of competent jurisdiction and proper venue within said State by service of process under the laws of said State and had lawfully been served with process in said State.

It is requested that a copy of any notice, process or pleading served hereunder be mailed to:

James H. Dayley
9840 West Main Street

Belleville, IL 62202

Dated: November 27, 1990

ABC Company
By: **[Signature]**
Title: **[x]**

By: **[Signature]**
Title: **[x]**

(Seal)

EXAMPLE OF A "TOMBSTONE" ADVERTISEMENT

This announcement does not constitute an offer to sell or the solicitation of an offer to buy the securities, which offer may be made only by means of an official Disclosure Document.

NEW ISSUE   _____ 1991

RESOURCE RECOVERY AND
MANUFACTURING CORP. ("RRMC")
9840 West Main Street, Belleville, Illinois 62202 • (618) 394-1365

160,000 Shares

Common Stock

Price: $6.25 Per Share

The Company's facility is designed to produce marketable
recycled products including a clean, uniformly-sized compost material
while reducing the waste stream by 50%.

*A copy of the Disclosure Document may be obtained by contacting the Company, Resource Recovery and Manufacturing Corp.,
9840 West Main Street, Belleville, Illinois 62202 • (618) 394-1365*

SAMPLE ESCROW AGREEMENT
(PUBLIC OFFERING)

This Agreement, dated April 18, 1991, by and between ABC Company (hereinafter referred to as "Issuer") and Local Bank (hereinafter referred to as the "Depository"). The Depository is located at West Main Street, Belleville, Illinois, 62223. The Issuer warrants that it has applied for authority from the Administrator of Securities of the State of Washington to sell certain securities and the Issuer intends that, if it is unable to sell securities in the sum of $750,000 by the 15th day of October, 1991, then the offering shall be terminated and the proceeds paid in by each of the subscribers shall be returned to them pursuant to this Agreement.

The Depository is willing to act as the depository hereunder.

In consideration of the mutual covenants and of other good and valuable consideration, the parties agree as follows:

1. The issuer shall deposit all monies received from the sale of securities in a special impound account in the depository to be designated the "ABC Company Account" (the "Impound Account"). The Issuer and its agents shall cause all checks received by it for the payment of securities to be

made payable to the Depository Impound Account. The Issuer agrees to include with the deposits made in the Impound Account a copy of each subscription agreement which shall include the name, address and social security or other tax identification number of each Subscriber and the date of each subscription. All funds so deposited shall be held in escrow by the Depository, shall not be subject to judgment or creditors claims against the Issuer unless and until released to said Issuer in accordance with this Agreement.

2. Unless the Administrator directs to the contrary, the funds deposited in the Impound Account may be invested as directed by the Issuer in bank certificates of deposit, United States government obligations or placed in an interest bearing savings account.

3. Deposits in the form of checks which fail to clear the bank upon which they are drawn, together with the related subscription agreement, shall be returned by the Depository to the Subscriber. A copy thereof shall be sent to the company.

4. If the funds deposited in the Impound Account amounts to or exceed $750,000 (the Minimum Subscription), the Issuer shall request the Depository to confirm the aggregate amount of deposit, the names of all subscribers and the amount deposited by each. the Issuer shall forward

the Depository confirmation to the Securities Administrator. The Depository shall continue to hold such funds and all other funds thereafter deposited with it hereunder until it has received a direction in writing from the Administrator instructing the Depository as to the disposition of the funds.

5. Upon receipt by the Depository of written notification signed by the Issuer advising that it was unable to sell the Minimum Subscription within the specific offering period, the funds deposited in the Impound Account shall be returned by the Depository to the Subscribers according to the amount each contributed. Total interest, less interest used to satisfy Depository costs and fees will be divided and returned to subscribers based upon the investment.

6. If, at any time prior to the disbursement of funds by the Depository as provided in Paragraph 4 or 5 of this Agreement, the Depository is advised by the Administrator that the registration to sell securities of the Issuer has been suspended or revoked, that any condition of its registration permit has not been met or that any provision of the Washington Securities laws have not been complied with, then the Administrator may direct the Depository not to disburse the proceeds contributed by the subscribers to the Issuer or may direct the Depository to refund the proceeds or

hold such proceeds until further notice by the Administrator.

7. This Impound Agreement shall terminate upon the disbursement of funds pursuant to Paragraph 4 or 5. Provided, however, the Issuer may abandon the public offering. Upon the receipt of a letter from the Issuer stating that the offering has been abandoned, copy to the Administrator, the Depository is authorized to return the monies received hereunder to the subscribers according to the amount each subscriber contributed with interest, less interest used to satisfy Depository costs and fees, and this Agreement shall terminate upon said distribution.

8. The sole duty of the Depository other than as herein specified, shall be to establish and maintain the Impound Account and to receive and hold the funds deposited by the company pursuant to all applicable banking laws and regulations of the State of Illinois.

9. The Issuer acknowledged that the Depository is performing the limited function of Depository and that this fact in no way means that the Depository has passed in any way upon the merits or qualification of, or has recommended, or given approval to, any person, security or transaction. A statement to this effect shall be included in the offering circular.

10. The Administrator may, at any time, inspect the records of the Depository, insofar as they relate to this Agreement, for the purpose of making any determination hereunder or effecting compliance with and conformance to the provisions of this Agreement.

11. The terms and conditions of this Agreement shall be binding on the heirs, executors and assigns, creditors or transferees, or successors in interest, whether by operation of law or otherwise, of the parties hereto. If, for any reason, the Depository named herein should be unable or unwilling to continue as such depository, then the Company may substitute, with the consent of the Administrator, another person to serve as Depository.

IN WITNESS WHEREOF, the parties have executed this Agreement the 18th day of April, 1991.

"ISSUER"
ABC COMPANY

By_____
   President

"DEPOSITORY"
LOCAL BANK

BY _____

ACKNOWLEDGED:

_____

Administrator of Securities
State of Washington

SUBSCRIPTION AGREEMENT

ABC COMPANY
West Main Street
Belleville, IL 62202

Gentlemen:

1. Terms of the Offering

ABC Company, an Illinois corporation ("Company")
has represented as follows:

1.1 The Shares are offered on a "best efforts"
120,000 Share minimum, 160,000 Share maximum basis
for a period of three hundred thirty (330) days,
commencing on the effective date of the Disclosure
Document (the "Termination Date"). Pending the
sale of the 120,000 Share minimum, all proceeds
will be promptly deposited into an escrow account
with Local Bank, Belleville, Illinois, Escrow Agent
for this offering. All Subscriptions will be made
payable to "LOCAL BANK, as Escrow Agent."

1.2 In the event the minimum number of Shares is
not sold within the Minimum Offering Period,
defined as the one hundred eighty (180) calendar
day period commencing upon the effective date of
the offering (unless extended up to an additional
ninety (90) calendar days at the option of the

Company), the offering will be withdrawn and the proceeds will be returned to subscribers without interest and without deduction for commissions or expenses. Subscribers will not be entitled to a return of funds from such escrow during the Minimum Offering Period. Once the 160,000 Shares have been sold, the Company will have a closing with respect to the minimum number of Shares and the Escrow Agreement will be terminated.

1.3 After the sale of the initial 120,000 Shares, the remaining 40,000 Shares will be offered on a "best efforts" basis until sold or the Termination Date, whichever is earlier. Subscriptions during this period will be payable to ABC Company.

2. Subscription.

2.1 The undersigned (the "Purchaser"), intending to be legally bound, hereby subscribes for common shares (the "Shares") of ABC, in the number of shares indicated in Section ___ hereof, at a purchase price of $6.25 per share.

2.2 The Purchaser will deliver payment directly to the Company together with completed copies of all applicable Subscription Documents.

2.3 The purchase price will be paid in accordance with the above Section 1, "Terms of the

Offering."

3. Representations and Warranties.

The Purchaser hereby represents and warrants to the Company as follows:

3.1 The Purchaser has been furnished and has carefully read: (a) the Disclosure Document relating to the Shares; and (b) the documents and other materials which are exhibits thereto or enclosed therewith or otherwise made available to the Purchaser, and understands the risks and other considerations relating to a purchase of Shares, including the risks set forth under the section captioned "Risk Factors" in the Disclosure Document.

[initial]

3.2 The Purchaser understands that the securities are being offered and sold in reliance on a specific exemption from the registration requirements of federal law.

[initial]

3.3 No oral or written representations have been made or oral or written information furnished to the Purchaser in connection with the offering of the Shares that are in any way inconsistent with the information stated in the Disclosure Document.

[initial]

3.4 The Purchaser, if executing this Subscription Agreement in a representation or fiduciary capacity, has full power and authority to execute and deliver this Subscription Agreement in such capacity and on behalf of the subscribing individual, partnership, trust, estate, corporation or other entity for whom or which the Purchaser is executing this Subscription Agreement;

[initial]

3.5 If the Purchaser is a corporation, the Purchaser is duly and validly organized, validly existing and in good tax and corporate standing as a corporation under the laws of the jurisdiction of its incorporation with full power and authority to purchase the Shares to be purchased by it and to execute and deliver this Subscription Agreement;

[initial]

3.6 If the Purchaser is a partnership, the representation, warranties, agreements and understandings set forth above are true with respect to all partners in the Purchaser (and if any such partner is itself a partnership, all persons holding an interest in such partnership, directly or indirectly, including through one or more partnerships), and the person executing this

Subscription Agreement has made due inquiry to determine the truthfulness of the representations and warranties made hereby;

[initial]

4. Acknowledgements.

The Purchaser is aware that:

4.1 The Company has minimal financial and operating history;

[initial]

4.2 The Purchaser recognized that investment in the Company involves significant risks and the Purchaser has taken full cognizance of and understands all of the risk factors related to the purchase of the securities, including but not limited to those set forth in the Disclosure Document.

[initial]

4.3 At least one state agency has had an opportunity to review the Disclosure Document and the merits of the Offering, and said state agency has passed upon the Shares and made a finding or determination as to the fairness or the justness of this transaction.

[initial]

4.4 The securities have not been registered under the Act, but have been registered under applicable state securities laws and by reason of an available exemption from the registration requirements of the Act may be sold, pledged, assigned or otherwise disposed of; and

[initial]

4.5 While the Shares will initially be listed on the Electronic Bulletin Board of the National Association of Securities Dealers Automated Quotation (NASDAQ) system, a market for the securities may not develop. Therefore, the Purchaser may bear the economic risk of the Purchaser's investment in the Company for an indefinite period of time.

[initial]

5. Acceptance of Subscription. The Purchaser hereby confirms that the Company has full right in its sole discretion to accept or reject the subscription of the Purchaser, provided that, if the Company decides to reject such subscription, the Company must do so promptly and in writing. In the case of rejection, any cash payments and copies of all executed Subscription Documents will be promptly returned (without interest or deduction in

the case of cash payments.) In the case of
acceptance, ownership of the number of Shares being
purchased hereby will pass to the Purchaser upon
registration of the transfer to the Purchaser by
the Company of a certificate or certificates
representing the Shares subscribed for, as further
described in an exhibit to the Disclosure Document.

[initial]

6. Indemnification. The Purchaser agrees to, and
hereby does, indemnify and hold harmless the
Company, its affiliates, the officers, directors,
partners, legal counsel, accountants and affiliates
of any thereof and each other person, if any, who
controls any thereof, within the meaning of Section
15 of the Act, against any and all loss, liability,
claim, damage and expense whatsoever (including,
but not limited to, any and all expenses reasonably
incurred in investigating, preparing or defending
against any litigation commenced or threatened or
any claim whatsoever) arising out of or based upon
any allegedly false representation or warranty or
breach of or failure by the Purchaser to comply
with any covenant or agreement made by the
Purchaser herein or in any other document furnished
by the Purchaser to any of the foregoing in
connection with this transaction.

[initial]

7. Irrevocability. The Purchaser hereby acknowledges and agrees, subject to the provisions of any applicable state securities laws providing for the refund of subscription amounts submitted by the purchaser, if applicable, that the subscription hereunder, is irrevocable and that the Purchaser is not entitled to cancel, terminate or revoke this Subscription Agreement and that this Subscription Agreement shall survive the death or disability of the Purchaser and shall be binding upon and inure to the benefit of the Purchaser and its respective heirs, executors, administrators, successors, legal representatives and assigns. In particular, the Purchaser shall not be entitled to return of his funds from Local Bank, Escrow Agent, during the Minimum Offering Period. If the Purchaser is more than one person, the obligations of the Purchaser hereunder shall be joint and several and the agreements, representations, warranties, and acknowledgements herein contained shall be deemed to be made by and be binding upon such person and each such person's heirs, executors, administrators, successors, legal representatives and assigns.

[initial]

8. Modification. Neither this Subscription Agreement nor any provisions hereof shall be waived, modified, discharged or terminated except

by an instrument in writing signed by the party against whom any such waiver, modification, discharge or termination is sought.

[initial]

9. Notices. Any notice, demand or other communication which any party hereto may be required, or may elect to give anyone interested hereunder shall be sufficiently given if: (a) deposited, postage prepaid, in a United States mail box, stamped registered or certified mail, return receipt requested, and addressed, if to the Company, to the address given in the preamble hereof, and, if to the Purchaser, to the address set forth hereinafter; or (b) delivered personally at such address.

[initial]

10. Counterparts. This Subscription Agreement may be executed through the use of separate signature pages or in any number of counterparts, and each of such counterparts shall, for all purposes, constitute an agreement binding on all parties, notwithstanding that all parties are not signatories to the same counterpart.

[initial]

11. Entire Agreement. This Subscription

Agreement contains the entire agreement of the parties with respect to the subject matter hereof, and there are no representations, warranties, covenants or other agreements except as stated or referred to herein.

[initial]

12. Severability. Each provision of this Subscription Agreement is intended to be severable from every other provision and the invalidity or illegality of the remainder hereof.

[initial]

13. Transferability; Assignability. This Subscription Agreement is not transferable or assignable by the Purchaser.

[initial]

14. Applicable Law. This Subscription Agreement and all rights hereunder shall be governed by, and interpreted in accordance with the laws of the State of Illinois.

[initial]

15. Subscription Information.
(To be completed by the Purchaser)

Number of Share subscribed for: **[#]** [a], at the

public offering price of $6.25 per share [b], in the form of cash in the amount of **[$]** ([a]) x [b]). PLEASE MAKE CHECKS DELIVERED IN RESPECT OF SUBSCRIPTIONS HEREUNDER PAYABLE TO "LOCAL BANK, AS ESCROW AGENT." After the Minimum Offering Period make checks delivered in respect of subscriptions hereunder payable to "ABC Company."

[initial]

Name (s) in which Share are to be registered

[x]
Print

[x]
Print

Form of joint ownership
(if applicable)

[   ]   Community Property
[   ]   Tenants-in-Common
[   ]   Joint Tenants with Rights of Survivorship
   If the Shares hereby subscribed for are to be owned by more than one person in any manner, the Purchaser understands and agrees that all of the co-owners of such Shares must sign this Subscription Agreement.

   IN WITNESS WHEREOF, the undersigned Purchaser(s)

do(es) represent and certify under the penalties of perjury that the foregoing statements are true and correct and that he has (they have) by the following signature(s) executed this Subscription Agreement this **[day]** day of **[month], [year]** .

[x]
[Signature]
Name of Purchaser
Signature of Purchaser

[x]
[Signature]
Name of Co-Purchaser
Signature of Co-Purchaser
(if any)

TYPE OF OWNERSHIP
(Check One)

[ ]   Individual (One signature required)
[ ]   Joint Tenants with right of Survivorship
(Both parties must sign)
[ ]   Tenants in Common (both parties must sign)
[ ]   Community Property (One signature required
if interest held in one name, i.e., managing
spouse, two signatures required if interest held in
both names)
[ ]   Trust (Please include copy of instrument
creating Trust)
[ ]   Corporation (Please include evidence of

authorization to purchase in form of resolutions or Articles of Incorporation and By-Laws)

[ ] Partnership (Please include copy of Partnership Agreement)

Please print here the exact name (registration) Purchaser desires for Shares

SIGNATURE PAGE FOR INDIVIDUAL PURCHASERS

Purchaser #1:	Purchaser #2:
[x]	[x]
Signature:	Signature:
[Signature]	[Signature]
SS#:	SS#:
[x]	[x]
Print or Type Name:	Print or Type Name:
[x]	[x]
Residence Address:	Residence Address:
[x]	[x]
Executed at:	Executed at:
Purchaser #1 (cont.):	Purchaser #2 (cont.)
[x]	[x]

this **[day]** day of   this **[day]** day of
[month],**[year]**   **[month]**, **[year]**

SIGNATURE PAGE FOR CORPORATE PURCHASES

[x]
Name of corporation (please print or type)

By **[signature]**
(Signature of authorized agent)
Title: **[x]**
Taxpayer Identification No.: **[x]**
Address of Principal Corporate Office **[x]**

Mailing Address, if different: **[x]**

Executed at:
[x]

SIGNATURE PAGE FOR TRUST PURCHASERS

[Signature]
Name of Trust (please print or type)
[Signature]
Name of Trustee (please print or type)
Date Trust was formed: **[x]**

By: **[Signature]**

Trustee's Signature

Taxpayer Identification No.: **[x]**

Trustee's Address: **[x]**

Executed at: **[x]**

SECTION FIVE

Selling Your Stock to the Public

As everyone knows, even the best product eventually has to be sold. If the U-7 Disclosure Documents' final revision and acceptance results in an "effectiveness letter" from the reviewing securities regulators, you are ready to start selling. This section tells you how to go about that task.

SELLING YOUR STOCK
TO THE PUBLIC

18

A MARKETING PLAN APPROACH

SCORs are slowly starting to be done. A book entitled, *"Take Your Company Public"* by Drew Field will be very helpful. This book is an outgrowth of Mr. Field's successful efforts over the past decade of helping companies take themselves public. His previous work was primarily with savings and loan associations changing from mutual status (owned by depositors) to stock companies (owned by shareholders). He is now turning his attention to SCOR candidate companies. For example, Mr. Field recently helped a catalog sales company complete a $1 million offering. The company sent an announcement to its better customers that they wanted to sell stock in their company and offered to send them the SCOR prospectus. The loyal customers wrote for the prospectus and invested in the company directly. Of course, the issue had to be cleared, (i.e., registered) in the 13 states that the offer and/or sale was made.

Here are the details of how Drew Field did the job.

The Real Goods Offering

John Schaeffer started this catalog direct marketing business with a $3,000 investment in 1986 and still owned it all. Half of its $6 million annual sales are in alternative energy generation (photovoltaic, wind, hydro systems) and energy conservation. The rest are a broad range of environmental, "green" products. Real Goods had all the elements for a DPO (Direct Public Offering) success:

1. The business would excite prospective investors, making them want to share its future.

2. There is a history of profitable operations under the company's present management.

3. The company and management meet standards of honesty, social responsibility and competency.

4. Share ownership makes sense for people without experience investing in small company shares.

5. The company has natural affinity groups with discretionary cash to risk for long-term gain.

6. Those affinity groups will recognize the company's name and consider its message.

7. Their names, addresses, telephone numbers and some demographics are in the company's data base.

He first selected customers who had done over a certain level of business, then sorted them by state. Thirteen states were picked for a $1 million SCOR offering, based upon the number of qualified customers and the cost of compliance with the securities laws.

A "tombstone" announcement and cover letter went to 15,000 customers in October, 1991. By January of 1992, there were 6,200 requests for the offering documents and 674 share owners. Another $300,000 had to be returned to 175 customers who subscribed after the maximum had been reached.

Real Goods has been accepted as the first company to be listed under the Pacific Stock Exchange program for SCOR companies. A specialist has been assigned and trading will begin after the SEC approves the PSE program.

How Do I Work With Stockbrokers to Help Sell the Offering?

It all depends on what you can work out. However, you must remember that none of the big firms will even want to talk to you on the subject. The SCOR offering, at the maximum, only amounts to 200,000 shares of a $5 stock -- a tiny offering to them. Therefore, you will have to get together with some rather small firms. Further, these little firms will not want to sell 10% or more of the issue because by doing so, they would then be classified as an "underwriter." There are major potential liabilities involved with being so designated. The insurance fees alone would cost them more than they could make if they sold out the whole issue!

Each small broker/dealer therefore could sell a maximum of 18,000 shares or $90,000 of your offering. Besides, their commission is going to be high, 15% or more.

The only way you can avoid going above the SCOR selling expense guidelines is to sell a major part of the deal yourself. That being the case, it would be smart to review the Washington state *"Consumer's Guide to Making Venture Investments in Small Business."* Approaching the sale of your stock from the investor's point of view will better prepare your sales team to properly manage that effort. By knowing your potential customers, you'll be ready to close the sale. Here are some topics, summarized from the above publication, that need to be considered from an investor's perspective.

Risks and Investment Strategy

The overriding principle that should control any decision to invest in a small business is: "Never make a venture investment that you cannot afford to lose entirely." Never use funds for a venture investment that might be needed for other purposes, such as college education, retirement, loan repayment, or medical expenses. Instead, use funds that would otherwise be used for a consumer purchase such as an extra vacation, or a down payment on a boat or RV.

Venture investments are sometimes structured as convertible debt. This doesn't mean that you should count on receiving the interest payments or even return of principal. This actually means it gives the investor a preferred claim over those of common and preferred stockholders if the company goes into bankruptcy or receivership, while preserving gain potential through the equity convertibility provision should the company prove successful.

Under no circumstances should you allow a securities salesperson (who is paid by commission) to convince you that the investment is not risky. Any such assurance is inaccurate. Venture investments are almost always highly illiquid even though the securities may technically be transferable. The fact is, you will usually be unable to sell your securities if the company takes a turn for the worse. Although the business may have registered or filed forms with a government agency, the agency has not evaluated or endorsed the investment. If anyone suggests that an investment will be successful because the agency has registered the offering or received forms on it, the individual may be guilty of a criminal offense.

Typically, the larger venture capitalists do not invest large portions of their money in a single company. Instead, they invest in a large number of companies and hope that a few highly successful investments will more than offset the unsuccessful ones. If you plan to invest large amounts of money in small businesses, you should consider this strategy. Even when using this strategy, do not invest funds you cannot afford to lose entirely. On the whole, the professional, experienced venture capitalist will have better luck with this system because they generally hear about the best deals before the general public.

Analyzing the Investments

Assuming that you have disposable income to spend on a venture investment, what factors would you consider when making an investment decision? Although there is no set formula for making successful investment decisions, certain factors are often considered particularly important by professional venture investors. They include:

1. Management
2. Industry
3. Marketing
4. Realizing a Return on Your Investment

Be aware that no matter how good the potential looks for future success, a lot usually goes wrong before a company is successful. Don't pay too much for securities in a company that lacks a history of operations that allows you to track some type of value. No matter how successful the company may be, the investment is not good if the price of the securities is too high.

Management

Most professional venture investors single out management quality as the most significant factor in the success of a small business. Inexperienced investors often give too much weight to a glamorous product and too little weight to management experience, skill, and integrity. The two most critical questions are:

- How much experience does management have as managers in the industry and in a small business?

- How successful were the managers in previous business?

Also, consider whether management is dealing unfairly with investors by taking salaries or other benefits that are too large in view of the company's stage of development.

Industry

The second most important factor to consider is the company's industry. A growth industry is desirable, but attention must also be paid to ease of entry and other competitive factors. Much key information concerning an industry is not usually included in a prospectus or other disclosure document. You may wish to make an in-depth investigation of the industry on your own. Industry research reports by securities analysts and statistics in trade journals may be useful.

Be careful when analyzing articles in the business press. These articles often reflect a singular view of companies in the industry and may contain exaggerated prospects. Also, when analyzing a new industry, do not confuse a "need" with a "market." Much advertising and expensive sales efforts may be required before customers even consider buying a product that meets a particular need.

Marketing

Do not overlook the cost of marketing and the time it takes to penetrate a market. A warning sign of market ignorance can be seen in a prospectus that estimates the total size of the market and then assumes that the company will somehow obtain some percentage of that market without actually analyzing what is involved to achieve that percentage.

The proper approach is to make a step-by-step analysis of the marketing strategies, efforts, and time required to penetrate a particular market segment, and to evaluate it with the company's available resources. This analysis will be more apt to provide a realistic assessment of market penetration than are percentages that are the result of guesswork.

Realizing a Return on Your Investment

A potential purchaser of a company's securities must anticipate the method by which investors are likely to ultimately realize a return on their investments. The two classic methods are resale in the public securities markets following a public offering or receiving cash or marketable securities in a merger or other acquisition of the company.

If the company is not likely to go public or be sold out within a reasonable time, it may not be a good investment regardless of its prospects for success. The outlook of being a minority security holder of a private company is generally frustrating. Management may receive a good return indefinitely through generous salaries and bonuses if the company is successful, but remains private. In addition, be leery of family businesses. Some businesses will never be candidates for public offerings. A careful review of the various types of companies that are public should give you insight as to whether a particular type of company is or is not a good prospect for an eventual public offering.

Other Suggestions

The disclosure document most often used in public venture offerings is Form U-7, which uses a question and answer format. The questions are designed to bring out particular factors that may be crucial to the proper assessment of the offering. The potential buyer should read each printed question and answer carefully. If an answer doesn't adequately address the issues raised by the question, reflect on the importance of that issue in the context of that particular company.

Remember, there are generally far more investment opportunities than there is venture money to go around. Even the best venture offerings are highly risky. If, after all your reviews, you're still not comfortable with the investment, the best decision is usually not to invest.

It's also a good idea to see management of the company face-to-face so you can effectively review management personnel. Focus on experience and track record rather than a smooth sales presentation. If at all possible, take a sophisticated business person with you to help you in your analysis.

Beware of information that is different from that in the disclosure document. If it is significant, it must be in the disclosure document or the offering will be illegal.

SECTION SIX

FUTURE CONSIDERATIONS

The landscape associated with the overall subject of this book is changing rapidly. In my opinion, these changes are for the better. Therefore, these next two chapters are my feelings as to the current potential use of the SCOR process. Don't fall into a trap of waiting to fill out your Form U-7 when the environment stabilizes. In reality, it probably never will.

19

SCORing Again

There needs to be an assessment by the entrepreneur as to whether his planned enterprise or existing company has better regional or national appeal. For those of a more regional appeal, it is my opinion that the entrepreneur would be better served in working with the securities divisions of his state to raise the money he needs for his business.

The determination of regional appeal has more to do with the marketability the stock of your enterprise has to investors than it does to the proximity of the state capital. Remember, it only takes

200 investors investing $5,000 each and you have the maximum amount that you can raise under the current program of SCOR.

The provisions of the SCOR program allow you to sell a maximum of $1 million worth in stock over a 12-month period. That means in 13 months after you complete the first offering you could be prepared to sell another $1 million.

Let's say you sold 20% of the company for $1 million in year number one and your success was solid. If you needed another $1 million you probably could sell only 10% of the company for that amount this time around. Why? Because your company will have established a good initial record of achievement which reduces the degree of risk to the investors. I'm sure you can see the benefit of raising more capital, as it is needed, using the SCOR process.

As of this printing, the following states have approved the SCOR Process: Alaska, Arizona, Connecticut, Idaho, Indiana, Iowa, Kansas, Maine, Massachusetts, Mississippi, Missouri, Montana, Nevada, North Carolina, North Dakota, Oklahoma, Pennsylvania, South Dakota, Tennessee, Texas, Vermont, Washington, Wisconsin, and Wyoming. Of this list, the securities personnel in the state of Washington have the most experience with and support for the SCOR program.

While each state is using the uniform disclosure documents, each also varies in the final requirements for approval. Some states, including Arizona and Texas, require people selling SCORs to take courses and pass special exams. It is of utmost importance to check with your state's requirements before jumping in with both feet. Get to know the regulator in your specific state (a list of the North American regulators is provided in the back of the book). This will make the process easier in the long run.

20

INTRODUCING
REGULATION "A" FILINGS

In layman's terms, Regulation A is a part of the Federal Securities laws that allows for the "simplified" filing of public stock offerings and other securities. It was a product of the growing consensus dealing with capital formation; namely, that it was unduly difficult for small businesses to raise money.

The SEC task force, organized in 1981 in conjunction with the **White House Conference on Small Business,** asked the question, "If Regulation A is available, why don't small businesses use it to raise capital?" The fact of the matter was that making a Regulation A filing was still quite complicated and expensive. Thus, Regulation A wasn't used as much as the SEC had hoped it would be -- especially by small businesses.

In the mean time, SCOR was introduced, along with its simplified filing document (U-7) and a $1 million cap.

With that in mind, the task force clearly understood that simply creating a way for deserving small companies to get a million dollars through SCOR wouldn't always be enough. There needed to be a way for those growing companies to raise even larger amounts on their way to becoming major companies. Therefore, during 1991 a deal was struck to have Regulation A filings be accomplished using the Form U-7 (like SCOR at the state level) and at a maximum size of $3 million. The target date for implementation was the end of 1991.

However, in August of 1991, the National Association of Securities Dealers (NASD) decided to implement a previously announced requirement for changing the qualifications for companies to be listed on NASDAQ, the electronic quote system run by the "club" called NASD. The NASD wanted to improve their product line.

The Over-The-Counter (OTC) Market is divided into four groups of stocks. The highest level is the National Market System which has all of the big actively-traded OTC companies like Apple Computer, Microsoft, Bank One, Intel, and Novell, to name a few. The next level down is the regular NASDAQ. The third level is called the "Bulletin Board." It started on a trial basis in 1991. The Bulletin Board is a list of small, seldom-traded stocks in a database format similar to what a serious computer user experiences when telephoning a database known as a bulletin board. The fourth level is referred to as the "Pink Sheets." It is a list of rarely-traded securities. It is printed on pink paper and is distributed to Broker/Dealer firms. The NASD wanted to take the lower capitalized stocks, those with fewer assets, off the regular NASDAQ and by so doing upgrade both levels two and three of the OTC Market. Thus, NASD changed the requirement for companies to be on the regular NASDAQ. The requirements were raised to $4 million in assets to get on and $2 million in assets to stay on. Previously, they were $2 million and $1 million respectively.

The goal of the task force and of the SEC was to have a way for companies to achieve greater ease in the trading of their stocks on NASDAQ and to use the U-7 Form for Regulation A filings. They clearly understood that rapidly emerging companies have a continual need to raise capital. Without access to such capital, their growth could be impeded. The NASD's changing of the entry level to $4 million threw that goal off track. It was back to the drawing boards!

While I was attending the 10th Annual Forum of the task force in the fall of 1991, the rumor circulating was that the upper limit for Reg A would be raised to $5 million. The estimated implementation date was supposed to be sometime in September of 1992.

As the drum beating of the presidential election year brought out cries of "JOBS, JOBS, JOBS," and "WE NEED TO GET CAPITAL INTO THE HANDS OF SMALL BUSINESSES," the target for approving the new Reg A deal accelerated. The new ceiling for Reg A was announced on March 11, 1992, along with several other actions (The details of proposed rule changes are covered in the Federal Register / Volume 57, Number 55 / Friday, March 20, 1992 / Proposed Rules).

Why did I tell you all this? This information was presented to let you know that there are, and will be viable alternatives for people who feel their companies need more than $1 million. Once they have proven their capacity to achieve stated objectives with lesser amounts, greater amounts will be available.

21

SUMMARY & CONCLUSIONS

So how does all of the material presented in this book apply to you as the owner of an entrepreneurial company that's trying to grow? As you already knew, growing requires money. What's been covered shows you that what you really need is CAPITAL. Hopefully, you now understand that you have some options for obtaining capital that you didn't have in the past.

For example, what if your well-run company needs around $3 million for the national roll-out of a new product? What's the best way to get it? There is no pat answer to this sort of question. However, one option might be to scale back your plans to what you can do for $1 million from a SCOR offering. Yet another possibility might be to do a $1 million SCOR this year followed by another $1 million SCOR issue thirteen months from now with another the following year. Still another option might be to use the Form U-7 as the disclosure document to do a Reg A offering at the federal level to get the whole $3 million.

Next, combinations of the above options might be considered. One might be to do a $1 million SCOR this year and then do a $2 million Reg A offering next year.

You and your advisors will just have to figure out what is the best approach for your situation and the correct timing involved.

As a fellow entrepreneur, I know that you've struggled with some of the various topics involved with the whole idea of *SCORing MILLIONS*. There's no extra charge for re-reading any sections of the book!

So what is your reaction to my ideas and instructions?

Some of you might feel that you and your company are not quite ready to embark upon such an effort. My comment to you is to not wait too long. Your competitor might be at the filing desk at the state capitol right now getting on with the process of getting $1 million with which he can fund his expansion to "beat the competition" (YOU!).

Others might feel that they wish they had known about SCOR several years ago, but right now you are being sought out by the big Wall Street firms to help fill your expansion capital needs. My parting words are only to wish you well and to express my hopes that your offering will be well-received.

For those of you who feel that you really want to try doing a SCOR, I'd like to hear from you as to how it goes. This whole SCOR landscape is changing rapidly. Networking with people who are out there "doing it" will help us all. Therefore, please feel free to leave a message on my voice mail. Just call me at 1-800-669-3964 and I will call you back.

Until then, "Good luck, entrepreneurs, wherever you are!"

22

SCOR CHECKLIST

In simplified terms, the following are the activities that need to be accomplished at the various stages of the SCOR process. Of course, these steps will vary from state to state.

1. Project Feasibility Assessment
Conduct independent management review
Determine if company can afford the project costs
Determine if the company's history is "clean"
Determine if the company can furnish audited financials

2. Commence Filling Out Form U-7
Start working on key questions (#2,3,4, 9, 29)
Determine the form, price and size of the offering
Determine how shares will be sold
Determine in which states to file
Start working on the other questions

3. Commence Rewrite and Editorial Review of . . .
Key questions
Other questions
Required Exhibits

4. Commence Assembly of . . .
Final SCOR document
Final exhibits
Legal opinion
Audited financial statements

5. File Registration With Selected States

6. Respond to the Comments of Selected States

7. Receive Permits to Sell the Offering

8. Complete the Minimum Sales

9. Break Escrow

10. Complete Offering

11. Complete Follow-up Activities With States

23

Q & A

In my work with entrepreneurs around the country, I find that the following questions are the ones that are most often asked about the SCOR process. Each should be carefully considered before becoming involved in a SCOR.

QUESTION #1: What happens to the stock held by current owners of the company when you do a SCOR?

Remember that the number of shares authorized can be increased, but the percent ownership stays the same when that happens. It's like having 10 dimes for a dollar. You still only have 100% of a dollar.

In a more simplified way of stating the situation, going public means investors pay dollars for pieces of paper that represent an ownership in the company. The magic involved here is that you can sell, say, 20% of your company and have the remaining 80% become worth more than the 100% was before! How? By the public confirming a "market value" of your company's shares.

Let's look at the situation with Real Goods in Chapter 18. John Schaeffer sold 7% of his company for $1,000,000. Does that mean the whole company is worth nearly $15 million ($1,000,000 divided by .07 equals $14,285,714.29)? Yes!

Now, could either John Schaeffer or Bill Gates of Microsoft sell all of their stock at one time? No. First, because the SEC wouldn't let them do so, and second, putting that much stock on the market at one time would depress the stocks. Why? Because, in spite of Congress' best efforts to do so, the law of supply and demand has not been repealed. Investors are buying into John Schaeffer and Bill Gates as part of the stock purchase. Without these company leaders around the investors' stock could be perceived as not being worth as much as it was before.

QUESTION #2: Why should doing a SCOR take so long? I got an SBA loan in three days.

Bob Ronstadt's quote of Joseph Schumpeter seems appropriate here: "We always plan too much and think too little."

Filling out the Form U-7 will force you to think, think, and think some more about your business in ways you would not have thought possible. Doing so will make you a better CEO. As the sports stars say, "No pain, no gain."

I feel that six months is about the correct amount of time you should plan on to complete a SCOR. Substantially less time than that probably means an inferior selling tool, i.e. -- the prospectus. In today's dynamic business environment, taking more than six months risks the material growing stale.

QUESTION #3: Now, tell me again. How much is a SCOR going to cost?

It all depends on how much of the total task you can do yourself. Don't forget, however, that your own time is not "free." You'll have to find a balance between doing the items you believe only you can do versus hiring a professional to help on other parts.

As a budget planning estimate, I would recommend that you allocate $100,000 to $120,000 to the overall project of doing a SCOR. Any part of the task that you and your staff can do will reduce that estimate range.

QUESTION #4: If I presently own 51% of my company, how can I do a SCOR and still maintain control?

You don't have to own 51% of your company to maintain control. For example, there is no doubt that Bill Gates, Jr. controls Microsoft even though he only owns about 35% of the company.

The board of directors controls a company and appoints a chief executive officer to carry out the policies and strategies "directed" by the board of directors.

As a practical matter, the present owners will have to give up some percentage of their ownership. Like a baseball trade, you have to give something to get something. The degree of "give-up" depends upon the perceived value the investor(s) places on a minority interest in your company.

Q & A

QUESTION #5: What's my company's balance sheet going to look like after I do a SCOR?

Let's take a look at the Real Goods case once again. First, the "Use of Proceeds," or Question 9 of the Form U-7, describes how management plans to use the net amount received from the offering. Real Goods planned to use about 28% of those funds to pay back short-term debt. That means that the amount of current liabilities will decrease as cash decreases.

Also, cash will decrease when about 12% of the offering amount is spent to purchase a new computer system, thereby increasing office equipment in the assets portion of the balance sheet.

Another item, 38% for working capital, starts out in the cash category and is expensed, some possibly for something tangible, but most of it goes to the various line items of the expense portion of the income statement.

Although a post-funding balance sheet is not required in the Form U-7, entrepreneurs and their accountants would be well advised to perform that exercise under various funding levels between the minimum and the maximum offering amounts.

QUESTION #6: You talk a lot about Washington state. What if I'm from another state?

I have acknowledged the help that the personnel at the securities division of Washington have been to me and other people who are starting to do SCORs. In a nutshell, they have just been involved with the process longer than other states. Regardless of that, you can sell your offering in any SCOR state. It just makes more sense to work with your state so you can sell to investors in your area.

QUESTION #7: What if my state isn't a SCOR state?

Start the SCOR process by going to your state securities division whether they are a SCOR state or not. From there on your actions will have to be guided by your particular location and planned selling region.

QUESTION #8: Let's say we've become "effective" to sell our company's stock issue. Now what do I do?

First, re-read Chapter 5 of Drew Field's book, *"Take Your Company Public."* Second, double check that you have satisfied any and all qualifications necessary to be able to sell your issue (schools, tests, etc.). Third, qualify each investor to be sure that this investment is appropriate for them. Fourth, present them with the disclosure document and insist that they read it. Fifth, after the investor has read the document, answer any and all questions by referring to the document itself and nothing that is not a part of it. Sixth, if the prospect wants to invest, in spite of all of your emphasis on the risks enumerated, he should sign the subscription agreement and send it with a check to the escrow agent you have chosen. Once you've collected the minimum amount specified you should check with the state so they can arrange for the release of funds in return for stock being issued.

QUESTION # 9: What's the deal on the planned offering price? What can it be?

The $5 per share price is the minimum. It can be more if you can justify it as part of the percentage of the company being sold. For example, a price of $5 per share combines with 200,000 shares to result in the $1,000,000 total. Correspondingly, a price of $6.25 per share implies that 160,000 shares are being offered for, again, $1,000,000.

QUESTION #10: My attorney is a great guy and has been very helpful in our general corporate affairs. However, he and his partners haven't helped "take a company public" before. What should I do if I want to investigate the SCOR process -- do it without him?

Everyone's situation is different, but in general, I'd recommend you have a frank discussion with your lawyer and agree upon a cost for him to become knowledgeable on the SCOR process. Of course, he could start by reading this book after you do. Remember, he's got a network of peers that will allow him to find the people to talk to and the material to read to learn all he needs to know about SCOR. You shouldn't have to pay for his total SCOR education which he can then apply to other clients without such costs.

QUESTION #11: What about my accountant? How much education is he going to need on SCOR?

Probably not that much considering the fact he's going to be submitting audited financials on your company. The various "accounting-type" questions in the U-7 will be pretty straight-forward for a CPA.

If, for a variety of possible reasons, you are going to have to change accountants to do a SCOR, I would recommend you seriously consider going with one of the "Big 6" accounting firms. They are all searching for up-and-coming client companies. Therefore, you should be able to negotiate a reduced fee structure. Having one of their names on the disclosure document will make it easier to sell.

QUESTION #12: What's the best way to determine which states to file in and when to do so?

I would recommend filing in each of your target states at approximately the same time. Laws do vary from state to state.

It's possible to be approved to sell in one while you're asked to adjust your disclosure document in another. Because your document must be consistent for every investor, you could be set up for several undesirable legal battles with your current investors, not to mention the individual state regulators.

Start out with a careful review of your potential investor list. Make your best estimate as to how much money each individual could spend on your offering. Now sort the list by "state of residence." The outcome will be a state-by-state list of potential investors and the estimated total sales per state.

The next step is to analyze where your time and effort would best be employed. It would, for example, probably not be worthwhile to go through the filing process and expense where you have two investors of $3000 each.

Once you've identified states where you feel there is good potential for the sale of your offering, arrange for a pre-offering conference with each one. That way you can sort out the differences and similarities between the various states securities laws relative to registration and the sale of securities. After this information gathering you can accurately prepare a disclosure document and a marketing plan which will respond to all of the targeted states thereby allowing you to essentially file with each one simultaneously.

QUESTION #13: Why wouldn't I start with a Reg A at the federal level and bypass the SCOR program at the state level?

It now appears you could, but I wouldn't recommend it. What I suggest you do is establish a good working relationship with your state regulators while going through the SCOR process. If you do so and really need another, say $2 million, in the following six months, it can be available. Just let performance lead the way rather than projections.

QUESTION #14: You say that the SCOR Program is best applied to an existing company. What would you suggest as a plan of attack for applying the SCOR process to a start-up or a near start-up business?

I've heard this question a lot since I've started to promote the SCOR process as an option for raising equity capital. Here's the way I advise people to proceed.

First of all, if you haven't already done so, you need to prepare a business plan. Until that's accomplished you're not an entrepreneur -- you're just a dreamer.

If you use the books and workbooks from Lord Publishing that I've recommended, you will have arrived at a point where you know if the business you're envisioning has the potential to be a multi-million dollar operation. Assuming that it does, SCOR might be something to get ready for in the future. You've determined that you can get started with a bare-bones operation for $150,000. If you don't have that much money, then you'll probably have to approach family and/or friends for the "seed money" you need. In Chapter 1 I advised you not to do that. What's changed?

The previous advice was given before you knew anything about SCOR. Now that you've been introduced to the SCOR Process, and have completed a comprehensive business plan, you are a very different entity. You can now offer what you probably couldn't have realistically proposed before; namely, a viable exit strategy for them to consider. Knowledgeable investors know that becoming involved in a business is easy. It's the"getting out" that's often quite difficult and traumatic to accomplish.

Your approach to investors would be to first explain what your business plan projects you have the potential for within five years.

You might figure these numbers assuming you do a SCOR funding of $1 million two years from now and a Reg A funding of $3 million during year four. At the present time you need the $150,000 private placement to get from your prototype product to a proof-of-concept manufacturing operation. The investors can decide to stay in, get out, or something in between, upon the eventual fundings. One idea might be to get their original investment back and let the remainder ride for possible appreciation in the future.

You will still have to go through the equation discussed in Chapter 5 to arrive at what "fair" percentage of the company the investors will be entitled to for their money.

By proceeding in the above fashion, you will be much better prepared to receive the necessary funding. The potential investors will perceive you as a much more qualified entrepreneur.

Q & A

24

STOP THE PRESSES!

In early March of this year I sat down with my publisher to discuss a target time frame for the release of this book. We agreed that late July/early August was a good initial goal. In mid-summer I learned that the 11th Annual SEC Government-Business Forum on Small Business Capital Formation was going to be held in early September versus later in the fall like it was the previous year. Furthermore, as we watched the election year's impact on the already increasingly dynamic environment of capital formation, it seemed appropriate to put off going to the printer until we could include a chapter on the happenings of the Forum.

So, here goes!

The normal two-day SEC Forum was preceded by a seminar on Small Business Capital Formation co-sponsored by the North American Securities Administrators Association (NASAA) and the State Bar Association of Arizona. The stated description of the seminar was as follows: Lawyers, securities regulators, and other professionals from throughout the country will participate in this one-of-a-kind program to learn the intricacies of the Small Corporate Offering Registration (SCOR), also known as the Uniform Limited Offering Registration (ULOR).

The four portions of the seminar covered the following topics:

1. The Small Corporate Offering Registration (SCOR)
2. The successful small corporate offering team
3. Selling the offering: The underwriter's responsibilities and commissions
4. Selling the offering: Communication with potential investors

As an indication of the increasing interest in the whole SCOR process, there were three times as many attendees at this year's seminar than there were at a similar event held just two years ago.

Because this seminar sought to give people unfamiliar with SCOR a foundation of understanding, much of the information was "ol' stuff" to a lot of the attendees and would have been to you, the reader, now that you've probably completed at least one read of this book. As is often the case in such gatherings, it's what you learn in the hallways and during the breaks, talking to your fellow attendees, that makes attending worthwhile.

The overriding challenge to the participants in both the SCOR seminar and the SEC Forum that followed is:

How can we foster the universally accepted need for the growth in capital formation and yet do so with adequate protection for the investing public?

For more than a decade, there has been a struggle to achieve an appropriate balance. Nevertheless, it's my strong opinion that each and every attendee was committed to meeting the above challenge and is earnestly engaged in finding the balance necessary to achieve practical application.

The SEC Forum is held in Washington, D.C. on odd-numbered years and at some other location around the country on even-numbered years. This year's was held in Scottsdale, Arizona. It followed the format which has evolved over previous years, namely two days consisting of:

Morning Session #1 -- A panel of experts followed by a question/answer period.

Morning Session #2 -- Testimonies from five previously identified and specially selected attendees (20 minutes each) making presentations from their various perspectives along with their recommendations for the total Forum to consider.

Afternoon Session -- Breakout group meetings where Forum attendees can discuss the recommendations coming from the expert panel presentation, the testifiers, or other items that individual attendees feel need to be considered.

The product produced by the forum each year is a set of recommendations to Congress for increasing small business capital formation. This is accomplished by a majority vote of the attendees.

The atmosphere at this year's Forum was unique. After years of making recommendations and seeing some encouraging progress, the attendees as a group seemed rather stunned with the magnitude of the SEC's Small Business Initiatives (SBI) proposed in March and implemented in August. We seemed to be reacting this year, trying to catch up to this more pro-active SEC attitude.

There were two issues that dominated the discussions and presentations over the three days. One was the "Test the Waters" provision of the SBI. The other was "How to Obtain Meaningful Liquidity for SCOR and Reg A Offerings." Let's discuss each one separately.

First, it's important to explain what the "Test the Waters" provision is and what it means to entrepreneurs. Wouldn't it be nice if you could know, or at least have some degree of confidence, that after you spent several months working on disclosure documents and getting them to pass muster with securities regulators, that people would buy your stock? Well, technically you couldn't do that as things stood prior to August, but the SEC now says you can. However, the states still say you can't.

Now, don't get excited about what could at first glance be seen as a Federal vs. States turf battle. The adhesive forces that keep ad hoc groups such as the SEC Forum glued together are still in force. The key players from all sides and disciplines have worked too hard for too long, and seen too much progress transpire, to let this great SBI pronouncement and implementation be lost now. The American Bar Association (ABA) and NASAA Study Group were very close, perhaps only days away, to a compromise with the SEC on what potential issuers of stock or other securities could and could not do to get a meaningful "indication of interest" from potential investors. This seemingly obstructive dilemma will be resolved soon in a manner with which everyone can live. There is just too much at stake for it not to happen. Everyone in every business knows that you have to find out through focus groups, surveys, interviews, etc. what the potential customer thinks about your product. So, if you and your company decide that SCOR is for you, don't delay work on your U-7 Questions. If you can't get the latest status on this issue from either your attorney or the state regulators with whom you're working, then give me a call on my voice mail at (800) 869-3840, and I'll call you back with the latest news as I know it.

As an example of "Testing the Waters," I took a galley copy (pre-printed before final paste-up) of this book to the Forum. As expected, it stirred up a lot of interest. Probably the most notable came from the representative of the Pacific Stock Exchange who said she'd have at least five referrals a day when the book was in print. In a similar fashion you, as a potential issuer of stock in your company, ought to be able to see how the public is going to react to your company or idea without getting yourself into legal trouble.

As I've been writing this final chapter, even better news has come my way. As of November 2, 1992, Colorado has become the first state to officially implement a "Testing the Waters" provision. I'm optimistic that other states will soon follow.

Now let's discuss "Liquidity." A statement came out of the SCOR seminar which seemed to carry on throughout the Forum.: "What we need are a few 'signature' SCOR issues!" What this means is having real-life companies that people can identify as having been through the SCOR process, and that have become successful. We're not there yet, but hopefully you and I will be part of making that happen.

All of the Forum participants are not sure how these SCOR

companies are going to be received by either the investing public or the broker/dealer community. There simply haven't been enough companies that have gone through the process. As I sat at the conference table in my breakout group discussing all the what-if's on this subject, I couldn't help but imagine a similar circumstance in my military career.

In my days as an electronic systems engineer for the Air Force, we were faced with a particularly vexing challenge. We needed to get the automatic flight control and terrain-following radar system on the big C-5 aircraft to work properly. The various engineering disciplines from the various contractors and sub-contractors, in conjunction with the test pilots from the contractors and the Air Force, came up with all types of ideas that might work to solve various parts of the overall problem. This reliability improvement group eventually came up with a configuration judged to be worth trying. A series of test flights was planned to see if it was truly practical. This series of test flights did not start out with a high difficulty mission such as a night flight through treacherous mountain terrain. Rather, it started out in broad daylight flying towards a single, small mountain with pilots poised to take immediate evasive action if the automatic system took the aircraft too close to the mountain. I was able to be on board one of those test flights. We were all watching closely as the pilots turned the aircraft onto a collision course with a mountain in Georgia and then engaged the automatic flight control system. As the plane approached the location where it should start its climb -- it did!

"Great! It works," we cheered from the cockpit. However, one flight does not a reliable system make. Each test flight that followed had to be flown before we could implement the prototype's changes into production instructions, which we eventually did.

I feel somewhat the same way about "testing" the SCOR process. It's time to go fly and see if what we've got here really works. If it does, liquidity will be a problem that is overcome by the events that will make SCOR companies successful. My advice to my group was that we should just "go fly" under the present restrictions of the SCOR environment with the goal to create some real "Signature Companies." If we do so, then the case will be resolved one way or another. However, with incomplete testing we'll never know. The real mission is to go fly your SCOR and find out if adequate liquidity develops as you're successful. Then you can come back for your next round of funding.

The following are a few miscellaneous news items that were of interest to potential SCOR companies:

• All the proposals made by the SEC in its SBI have been implemented. For example, Regulation A registrations can now be filed using Form U-7 for a maximum of $5 million.

• The Pacific Stock Exchange has amended its request for SEC approval to probationally list $1 million SCOR issues to also include Reg A issues.

• SBA controlled SBIC's are to become much more viable capital formation vehicles under legislation (HR 4111) signed by President Bush on September 4, 1992.

• A broker/dealer network has been formed in Arizona with the specific aim to do Reg A and possibly some SCOR offerings. They are offering to help form such networks in other states, if asked.

Further initiatives are also being considered by the SEC including raising the SCOR maximum to $3 million and the Reg A maximum to $10 million.

I'll wrap up this report with a story from the panel of experts on the second day of the SEC Forum. The moderator of the panel asked the members of the audience to contemplate how they would have felt about a proposal asking them to fund a company in 1985 that involved producing useful products derived from mushrooms and algae. The business was composed of three people who were leaving a big firm and had never run a company on their own. Take some time to think about your answer before reading any further.

You might now wish that you had been able to invest in that company. It's called Martek and it's in the bio-tech industry. It now has 50 employees and did $4 million in sales last year. It has raised over $8 million in a series of fundings from state and private sources. The last round of funding gives the company a total corporate value of $50 million. It now has viable products in the areas of specialized nutrition, pharmaceuticals, pharmaceutical testing compounds and non-intrusive diagnostic testing procedures.

I'm not saying that this company could have used either the SCOR or a Reg A registration and achieved the same results. However, they might have been viable alternatives. That is why it is such a special time for entrepreneurs. You can now evaluate the SCOR and/or Reg A alternatives where Martek didn't have such options available in 1985.

As is often the case, timing is everything.

NORTH AMERICAN REGULATORS

North American Securities Administration Association, Inc.

Administrators

Alabama
Mr. Robert L. Rash
Director
Securities Commission
770 Washington Avenue, Suite 570
Montgomery, Alabama 36130
205-242-2984

Alaska
Mr. Lawrence P. Carroll
Senior Securities Examiner
Dept. of Commerce & Economic Development
Division of Banking, Securities, & Corporations
PO Box 110887
Juneau, Alaska 99811-0807
907-465-2521

Alberta
Mr. Ronald Will
Chairman
Securities Commission
4th Floor, 300 - 5th Avenue S.W.
Calgary, Alberta
T2P 3C4 Canada
403-297-4277

Arizona
Mr. Dee Harris
Director of Securities
Corporation Commission
Securities Division
1200 West Washington, Suite 201
Phoenix, Arizona 85007
602-542-4242

Arkansas
Mr. Joe E. Madden
Commissioner
Securities Department

Heritage West Building
201 East Markham, 3rd Floor
Little Rock, Arkansas 72201
501-324-9260

British Columbia
Mr. Wade Nesmith
Superintendent of Brokers
Securities Commission
865 Hornby Street, 11th Floor
Vancouver, British Columbia
V6Z 2H4 Canada
604-660-4800

California
Mr. Thomas Sayles
Commissioner
Department of Corporations
3700 Wilshire Boulevard, Suite 600
Los Angeles, California 90010
213-736-2741

Colorado
Mr. Philip A. Feigin
Securities Commissioner
Division of Securities
1580 Lincoln, Suite 420
Denver, Colorado 80203
303-894-2320

Connecticut
Mr. Ralph A. Lambiase
Director
Department of Banking
Securities & Business Investments Division
44 Capitol Avenue
Hartford, Connecticut 06106
203-566-4560

Delaware
Mr. Richard W. Hubbard
Securities Commissioner
Department of Justice
Division of Securities
State Office Building
820 North Frence Street, 8th Floor
Wilmington, Delaware 19801
302-577-2515

District of Columbia
Mr. James F. Whitescarver, Jr.
Director of Securities
Securities Commission
450 5th Street N.W., Suite 821
Washington, D.C. 20001
202-626-5105

Florida
Mr. Don Saxon
Director
Office of Comptroller

Department of Banking and Finance
The Plaza, The Capitol
Tallahassee, Florida 32399
904-488-9805

Georgia
Mr. Verley J. Spivey
Deputy Secretary of State
Office of the Secretary of State
Division of Business Services & Regulation
2 Martin Luther King, Jr. Drive
Suite 315, West Tower
Atlanta, Georgia 30334
404-656-2894

Hawaii
Ms. Lynn Wakatsuki
Commissioner of Securities
Department of Commerce & Consumer Affairs
PO Box 40
Honolulu, Hawaii 96810
808-586-2744

Idaho
Mr. Wayne Klein
Securities Bureau Chief
Department of Finance
Securities Bureau
700 West State Street
Boise, Idaho 83720
208-334-3684

Illinois
Mr. Arthur Telcser
Director
Office of the Secretary of State
Securities Department
900 South Spring Street
Springfield, Illinois
217-782-2256

Indiana
Ms. Miriam Smulevitz Dant
Commissioner
Office of the Secretary of State
Securities Division
302 West Washington, Room E-111
Indianapolis, Indiana 46204
317-232-6681

Iowa
Mr. Crain A. Goettsch
Superintendent of Securities
Insurance Division
Securities Bureau
Lucas State Office Building
Des Moines, Iowa 50319
515-281-4441

Kansas
Mr. Jim Parrish
Securities Commissioner

Office of Securities Commissioner
618 South Kansas Avenue, 2nd Floor
Topeka, Kansas 66603
913-296-3307

Kentucky
Mr. Ed Hatchett
Director
Department of Financial Institutions
Division of Securities
911 Leawood Drive
Frankfort, Kentucky 40601
502-564-3390

Louisiana
Mr. Harry C. Stansbury
Deputy Securities Commissioner
Securities Commission
CNG Tower, Suite 420
1450 Poydras Street
New Orleans, Louisiana 70112
504-568-5515

Maine
Mr. Stephen L. Diamond
Securities Administrator
Department of Professional & Financial Regulation
Bureau of Banking
Securities Division
State House Station 121

Augusta, Maine 04333
207-582-760

Manitoba
Mr. G. Derwood Walker, Q.C.
Chairman
Securities Commission
1128-405 Broadway Avenue
Winnipeg, Manitoba
R3C 3L6 Canada
204-945-2548

Maryland
Ms. Ellyn L. Brown
Securities Commissioner
Office of the Attorney General
Division of Securities
200 St. Paul Place, 20th Floor
Baltimore, Maryland 21202
410-576-6360

Massachusetts
Mr. Barry C. Guthary
Director
Securities of the Commonwealth
Securities Division
J.W. McCormack Building
One Ashburton Place, 17th Floor
Boston, Massachusetts 02108
617-727-3548

Mexico
Mr. Luis Miguel Moreno Gonez
Presidente
Comision Nacional de Valores
Barranaca del Muerto No. 275
Col. San Jose Insurgentes Colonia
Mexico, 03900, D.F.
011-525-550-9756

Michigan
Mr. Carl L. Tyson
Director
Department of Commerce
Corporation & Securities Bureau
6546 Mercantile Way
Lansing, Michigan 48909
517-334-6212

Minnesota
Mr. Bert McKasy
Commissioner of Commerce
Department of Commerce
133 East Seventh Street
St. Paul, Minnesota 5101
612-296-2594

Mississippi
Ms. Susan A. Shands
Assistant Secretary of State
Office of the Secretary of State
Securities Division

PO Box 136
Jackson, Mississippi 39205
601-359-6371

Missouri
Mr. John R. Perkins
Securities Commissioner
Office of the Secretary of State
600 West Main Street
Jefferson City, Missouri 65101
314-751-4136

Montana
Ms. Andrea "Andy" Bennett
State Auditor & Securities Commissioner
Office of the State Auditor
Securities Department
PO Box 4009
Helena, Montana 59604
406-444-2040

Nebraska
Mr. Jack E. Herstein
Assistant Director
Department of Banking & Finance
Bureau of Securities
PO Box 95006
Lincoln, Nebraska 68509
402-471-3445

Nevada
Mr. Mark J. Griffin
Deputy Secretary of State
Office of the Secretary of State
Securities Division
1771 East Flamingo Road, Suite 212B
Las Vegas, Nevada 89158

New Brunswick
Mr. Donne W. Smith, Jr.
Administrator
Securities Act
PO Box 5001
St. John, New Brunswick
E2L 4Y9 Canada
506-658-3060

Newfoundland
Mr. George F. Kennedy
Director of Securities
Department of Justice
Confederation Building, PO Box 8700
St. Johns, Newfoundland
A1B 4J6 Canada
709-729-4189

New Hampshire
Mr. Thomas B. Connolly
Assistant Secretary of State
Bureau of Securities Regulation
Department of State

State House, Room 204
Concord, New Hampshire 03301
603-271-1463

New Jersey
Mr. A. Jared Silverman
Chief
Department of Law & Public Safety
Bureau of Securities
Two Gateway Center, 8th Floor
Newark, New Jersey 07102
201-504-3600

New Mexico
Ms. Nancy Smith
Director
Regulation and Licensing Department
Securities Division
725 St. Michaels Drive
Santa Fe, New Mexico 87501
505-827-7140

New York
Ms. Alice McInerney
Assistant Attorney General
Department of Law
Bureau of Investor Protection & Securities
120 Broadway, 23rd Floor
New York, New York 10271
212-416-8000

North Carolina
Mr. Eugene J. Cella
Deputy Securities Administrator
Office of the Secretary of State
Securities Division
300 North Salisbury Street, Room 404
Raleigh, North Carolina 27611
919-733-3924

North Dakota
Mr. Glenn A. Pomeroy
Securities Commissioner
Office of the Securities Commissioner
600 East Boulevard
Bismark, North Dakota 58505
701-224-2910

Northwest Territories
Mr. Gary MacDougall
Registrar of Securities
Government of the Northwest Territories
PO Box 1320
Yellowknife, Northwest Territories
X1A 2L9 Canada
403-873-7490

Nova Scotia
Mr. Robert B. MacLellan
Chairman
Nova Scotia Securities Commission

1690 Hollis Street
Halifax, Nova Scotia
B3J 3J9 Canada
902-424-7768

Ohio
Mr. Mark V. Holderman
Commissioner of Securities
Division of Securities
77 South High Street
Columbus, Ohio 43215
614-644-7381

Oklahoma
Mr. Irving L. Faught
Administrator
Securities Commission
Department of Securities
PO Box 53595
Oklahoma City, Oklahoma 73152
405-521-2451

Ontario
Mr. Joe Oliver
Executive Director
Securities Commission
20 Queen Street West, Suite 1800
Toronto, Ontario
M5H 3S8 Canada
416-597-0681

Oregon
Ms. Nancy Burke
Acting Securities Administrator
Department of Insurance & Finance
Securities Section
Labor & Industries Building
Salem, Oregon 97310
503-378-4387

Pennsylvania
Mr. Robert M. Lam
Chairman
Securities Commission
Eastgate Office Building
1010 North 7th Street, 2nd Floor
Harrisburg, Pennsylvania
717-787-8061

Prince Edward Island
Mr. Merrill H. Wigginton
Registrar of Securities
Department of Justice
Securities Act
105 Rochford Street
Charlottetown, Prince Edward Island
C1A 7N8 Canada
902-368-4550

Puerto Rico
Mr. Asdrubal Aponte
Acting Securities Commissioner

Office of the Commissioner of Financial Institutions
Government Employees Retirement Fund Building
437 Ponce de Leon Avenue, 14th Floor
Hato Rey, Puerto Rico 00918
809-751-5606,7837

Quebec
Mr. Roland Cote
Commissioner
Commission Des Valeurs Mobillieres du Quebec
800 Square Victoria, 17th Floor
PO Box 246, Stock Exchange Tower
Montreal, Quebec
H4Z 1G3 Canada
514-873-5326

Rhode Island
Mr. Michael Fines
Associate Director & Superintendent of Securities
Department of Business Regulation
Securities Division
233 Richmond Street, Suite 232
Providence, Rhode Island 02903-4232
401-277-3048

Saskatchewan
Mr. Marcel de la Gorgendiere, Q.C.
Chairman
Securities Commission
1914 Hamilton Street, #850
Regina, Saskatchewan

S4P 3V7 Canada
306-787-5645

South Carolina
Mr. Bernet R. Maybank III
Deputy Securities Commissioner
Department of State
Securities Division
1205 Pendleton Street, Suite 501
Columbia, South Carolina 29201
803-734-1087

South Dakota
Ms. Debra M. Bollinger
Director
Division of Securities
910 East Sioux Avenue
Pierre, South Dakota 57501
605-773-4823

Tennessee
Mr. Kenneth McClellan
Assistant Commissioner-Securities
Department of Commerce & Insurance
Securities Division
Volunteer Plaza, Suite 680
500 James Robertson Parkway
Nashville, Tennessee 37243
615-741-5911

Texas
Mr. Richard D. Latham
Securities Commissioner
State Securities Board
PO Box 13167
Austin, Texas 78711-3167
512-474-2233

Utah
Mr. Earl S. Maeser
Director
Department of Commerce
Securities Division
PO Box 45808
Salt Lake City, Utah 84145-0808
801-530-6955

Vermont
Ms. Elizabeth Costle
Deputy Commissioner of Securities
Department of Banking, Insurance & Securities
Securities Division
120 State Street
Montpelier, Vermont 05620-3101
802-828-3420

Virginia
Mr. Lewis W. Brothers, Jr.
Director
State Corporation Commission
Division of Securities & Retail Franchising

1220 Bank Street, 4th Floor
Richmond, Virginia 23209
804-786-7751

Washington
Mr. Jack Beyers
Administrator
Department of Licensing
Securities Division
PO Box 9033
Olympia, Washington 98507-9033
206-753-6928

West Virginia
Mr. Jack Hall
Deputy Commissioner and Division Director
State Auditor's Office
Securities Division
State Capitol Building
Charleston, West Virginia 25305
304-348-2257

Wisconsin
Mr. Wesley L. Ringo
Securities Commissioner
Office of the Commissioner of Securities
111 West Wilson Street
PO Box 1768
Madison, Wisconsin 53701
608-266-3431

Wyoming
Ms. Kathy Karpen
Secretary of State & Securities Commissioner
Secretary of State
Securities Division
State Capitol Building
Cheyenne, Wyoming 82002
307-777-7370

Yukon Territory
Mr. Richard Roberts
Registrar of Securities
Department of Justice
Justice Services Division, Corporate Affairs
PO Box 2703
Whitehorse, Yukon Territories
Y1A 2C6 Canada
403-667-5005

SUGGESTED READING

The following is a list of books I used in my research for this book and in my continuing education for SCOR and other related topics. Each is highly recommended if you are planning to take a company public in the future.

Entrepreneurial Finance
Taking Control of Your Financial Decision Making
By Robert Ronstadt, Lord Publishing, Inc., 1988.

Written by an entrepreneurship professor who has been out "doing it" in the real world.

Venture Feasibility
Planning Your First Step Before Writing a Business Plan
By Robert Ronstadt and Jeffrey Shurman, Lord Publishing, Inc., 1988.

It's just what its title says.

The Business Plan
A State-of-the-Art Guide
By Michael O'Donnell, Lord Publishing, Inc., 1988.

This is Lord Publishing's companion to the previous book.

Pratt's Guide to Venture Capital Sources
Edited by Jane K. Morris and Susan Isenstein, published annually by Venture Economics, Inc.

The recognized "Bible of Venture Capital" -- what it is, how it works, who the players are and how to contact them.

Venture Capital Handbook: An Entrepreneur's Guide to Obtaining
Capital to Start a Business, Buy a Business, or Expand an Existing
Business
By David Gladstone, Prentice Hall, 1988.

The author describes in great detail how to prepare for and negotiate with the venture capital community.

Take Your Company Public
The Entrepreneur's Guide to Alternative Capital Sources
By Drew Field, New York Institute of Finance Corp., Simon &
Schuster, 1991.

The author provides details about how the market for selling
stocks has changed over the years and how today's entrepreneur can
sell stock in his company direct to the public.

Cashing Out
The Entrepreneur's Guide to Going Public
By James B. Arkebauer with Ron Schultz, Harper Business, 1991.

If *SCORing MILLIONS* comes out as "How to Go Public -- 101,"
then this book might be considered as "Course 401." It will be very
helpful for the entrepreneur to read once he's embarked upon the
SCOR process.

The Great Game of Business
The Only Sensible Way to Run a Company
By Jack Stack, Doubleday Currency, 1992.

If you will apply the exciting methods and principles wonderfully
explained by the author to your business, it will be well worth
going public.

Thriving Up and Down the Free Market Food Chain
By Arthur Lipper III with George Ryan, Harper Business, 1991.

A compilation of experiences, opinions, and recommendations from a
a master entrepreneur.

Thriving on Chaos
Handbook for a Management Revolution
By Tom Peters, Alfred Knopf, 1987.

It is indeed "THE Management Handbook" for anyone considering doing a SCOR.

Glossary From the New York Stock Exchange

This pamphlet covers the investment language that may sound strange to a newcomer in the world of public finance.

INDEX

American Bar Association (ABA): 279-281
Apple Computer: 74-75, 258
Articles of Incorporation: 123

Bank loans: Chapter 2
Blind pools: Chapter 7, 107
Body Shop International: 97
Bogle & Gates: 80
Bourne, Randall: 29-31, 41
Bush, George: 49, 283

Business plan: 43, 113-115, 120, 274

Checklist for SCOR: Chapter 22
Chief Financial Officer (CFO): 91, 119
Comments letter: 107
"Consumer's Guide to Making Venture Investments in Small Business": 246
Crandell, George: 59

Debt: 38-39, 48, 124, 246, 270
Digital Equipment Company: 62
Dilution: 96, 111
Direct Public Offering (DPO): 244
Disclosure Document: 104-105, 114, 124, 249-251, 262, 271-273, 280-281, 283

"Entrepreneurial Finance": 59
Equity: 28, 38-39, 47-49, 55-56, 97, 246, 274
Escrow Agreement: 124, 220
Exposures, Inc.: 41

Federal Express: 74
Field, Drew: 243-244, 271
Forbes: 97
Form U-2: 124, 215
Form U-2A: 124, 215
Form U-7: 81, 105-107, 109-110, 123, Chapter 16-17, 250, 253, 258-259, 262, 266, 268, 270, 272, 281, 283
Form U-7 Exhibits: Chapter 17
Form U-7 Instructions: Chapter 16

Gates, Bill: 268-269
Gladstone, David: 59
Government-Business Task Force on Small Business Capital
    Formation: 78-79, 81, 257-259

Hewlett-Packard: 74-75
Hines, James E.: 115

Initial Public Offering (IPO): Chapter 6, 80
Investment banking: 57, 66

Kasten Group, Inc.: 55

Leveraged buy-outs: 57
Liles Jr., Mike: 80-81
Limited Offering Exemption (LOE-82): 81
Liquidity: 52, 80, 96, 280-283
Loans: 38, 45, 74, 76

Martek: 284
McDonald's: 74
Money Market Mutual Funds: 31-32, 75

NASDAQ: 231, 258-259
National Association of Securities Dealers (NASD): 206, 210,
    258-259
National Market System: 258
New York Stock Exchange: 75
Nike: 74

North American Securities Administrators Association (NASAA): 278, 280-281

Olson, Ken: 62
Over-the-Counter (OTC) market: 75, 258

Pacific Stock Exchange (PSE): 96, 245, 281, 283
Pei, I.M.: 115
Penny stock: 68, 79
"Pratt's Guide to Venture Capital": 57
Private placements: Chapter 4
Public shells: Chapter 7

Reagan, Ronald: 48, 77
Real Goods: 245, 268, 270
Regulation A (Reg A): Chapter 20, 273, 275, 280, 283-284
Resume: 120-121
RJR Nabisco: 57
Ronstadt, Robert: 59
Rule 504 of Regulation D: 128, 133, 205

SBA loans: Chapter 2
Schaeffer, John: 244, 268
Schumpeter, Joseph: 268
Securities and Exchange Commission (SEC): 78-79, 81, 96-97, 245, 257-259, 268, 277-279, 280, 283-284
Seed capital: 56
Seed investors: 43
Seed money: 274
Selling Agency Agreement (Form U-1): 123, 205
Service Corps of Retired Executives (SCORE): 48

Silicon Valley: 77
Small Business Administration (SBA): Chapter 3, 283
Small Business Investment Companies (SBIC's): 48-49, 283
Smith, Ralph: 80
States approved for SCOR: 256
Stock Market: 74, 79
Stock Market Crash: 100
Stockbrokers: 92, 245
Stockholders: 39, 93, 97, 111, 125, 246
Subscription Agreement: 125, 226, 271

"Take Your Company Public": 243, 271
"Tombstone" announcement: 124, 138, 219, 245

Underwriter: 92, 245
Uniform Limited Offering Registration (ULOR): 28, 80, 278

Venture capital (VC): 46, 48, Chapter 5
Venture capital funds: 57
"Venture Capital Handbook": 59
"Venture Feasibility Planning Guide": 113

Wal-Mart: 74
White House Conference on Small Business: 77, 257

INDEX

ABOUT THE AUTHOR

James Dayley is currently a venture capital associate with Corporate Capital Resources, Inc. He specializes in helping small businesses obtain up to $1 million in public equity funding, primarily through the SCOR program.

As a regular participant at the U.S. Securities and Exchange Commission's Annual Government-Business Forums on Small Business Capital Formation, he is an active participant in the political processes needed to support movements for greater capital availability for small business ventures.

He is an experienced financial consultant and one of a pocket of individuals who is driven to bring the SCOR message into the mainstream. Dayley has held jobs for C.A. Kasten & Associates in business acquisitions and E.F. Hutton as a financial planner for private companies.

His diverse background also includes retiring from the U.S. Air Force with the rank of Lieutenant Colonel. His responsibilities included the command of special communications units in support of high priority missions worldwide.